'Prior to Covid-19, flexible working was, to most people, a largely theoretical construct that applied to a very limited number of employees in specific circumstances. That all changed very quickly and now most people in jobs that can be done remotely have experienced some form of flexible working. As we now move into a more defined state of hybrid working, this excellent book provides meaningful and actionable insights into the challenges, opportunities and potential pitfalls that lie ahead. I thoroughly recommend it to anyone dealing with this issue in their workplace.'
David Roomes, Chief Medical Officer, Rolls-Royce

'*Remote Workplace Culture* is spot-on for the new world of work! This cutting-edge contribution for HR professionals and hybrid-working professionals is a rich resource to address all aspects of the human side of working, achieving, and contributing to make an impact without burning out and while staying healthy.'
James Campbell Quick, Professor Emeritus, The University of Texas at Arlington

'Covid-19 has shaken up the world of work and the workplace for many people. This book is invaluable for employers and employees alike as we navigate how and where we work and our life–work balances of the future. Fascinating, timely, informative and highly readable.'
Rita Gardner CBE, CEO, Academy for the Social Sciences

'This is vintage stuff from Sir Cary Cooper and Sean O'Meara. Rich with examples and reassuring in its tone, they navigate an exciting new world of change and opportunity. Essential reading for anyone interested in tomorrow.'
Chris Lewis, CEO and Chairman, LewisPR

Remote Workplace Culture

How to bring energy and focus to remote teams

Sean O'Meara

Cary Cooper

KoganPage

First published in Great Britain and the United States in 2022 by Kogan Page Limited

2nd Floor, 45 Gee Street London EC1V 3RS United Kingdom	8 W 38th Street, Suite 902 New York, NY 10018 USA	4737/23 Ansari Road Daryaganj New Delhi 110002 India

www.koganpage.com

© Sean O'Meara and Cary Cooper, 2022

The rights of Sean O'Meara and Cary Cooper to be identified as the authors of this work have been asserted by them in accordance with the Copyright, Designs and Patents Act 1988.

ISBNs

Hardback	978 1 3986 0388 2
Paperback	978 1 3986 0386 8
Ebook	978 1 3986 0387 5

British Library Cataloguing-in-Publication Data
A CIP record for this book is available from the British Library.

Library of Congress Cataloging-in-Publication Data
Names: O'Meara, Sean, author. | Cooper, Cary L., author.
Title: Remote workplace culture: how to bring energy and focus to remote teams / Sean O'Meara and Cary Cooper.
Description: London; New York, NY: Kogan Page, 2022. | Includes bibliographical references and index.
Identifiers: LCCN 2021057391 (print) | LCCN 2021057392 (ebook) | ISBN 9781398603868 (paperback) | ISBN 9781398603882 (hardback) | ISBN 9781398603875 (ebook)
Subjects: LCSH: Virtual work teams. | Telecommuting. | Corporate culture.
Classification: LCC HD66 .O464 2022 (print) | LCC HD66 (ebook) | DDC 658.4/022–dc23/eng/20211201
LC record available at https://lccn.loc.gov/2021057391
LC ebook record available at https://lccn.loc.gov/2021057392

Typeset by Integra Software Services, Pondicherry
Print production managed by Jellyfish
Printed and bound by CPI Group (UK) Ltd, Croydon, CR0 4YY

Dedicated to the memory of Kim O'Meara, a remote working inspiration who, from her spare bedroom, helped more than 60,000 dogs find permanent homes.
www.dogsblog.com/kim-omeara/

CONTENTS

ABOUT THE AUTHORS

SEAN O'MEARA

Sean O'Meara is a public relations and user experience consultant from Nottinghamshire, England. He founded the 'remote-first' digital communications consultancy Essential Content in 2015 and has more than 15 years' experience of working remotely. He lives in Stockport, England.

PROFESSOR SIR CARY COOPER CBE

Cary L Cooper is the 50th Anniversary Professor of Organizational Psychology and Health at Manchester Business School, University of Manchester. He is a founding President of the British Academy of Management, President of the Chartered Institute of Personnel and Development (CIPD), former President of RELATE and President of the Institute of Welfare. He was the Founding Editor of the *Journal of Organizational Behavior*, former Editor of the scholarly journal *Stress and Health* and is the Editor-in-Chief of the Wiley-Blackwell *Encyclopaedia of Management*, now in its 3rd edition.

He has been an adviser to the World Health Organisation, ILO and EU in the field of occupational health and wellbeing, was Chair of the Global Agenda Council on Chronic Disease of the World Economic Forum (2009–10) then served for five years on the Global Agenda Council for mental health of the WEF and was Chair of the Academy of Social Sciences (2009–15). He was Chair of the Sunningdale Institute in the Cabinet Office and National School of Government (2005–10). Professor Cooper is currently the Chair of the National Forum for Health and Wellbeing at Work, comprised of 40 global companies including BP, Microsoft, NHS Executive, the UK government (wellbeing lead), Rolls-Royce and John Lewis Partnership.

Professor Cooper is the author/editor of over 250 books in the field of occupational health psychology, workplace wellbeing, women at work and occupational stress. He was awarded the CBE by the Queen in 2001 for his contributions to occupational health and in 2014 he was awarded a Knighthood for his contribution to the social sciences.

Introduction

Tejas Patel had been in the same line of work for nearly forty years. He'd steadily progressed through the ranks of his profession, and as he approached the fifth decade of his career he occupied a senior position and was widely respected by his peers.

In 2019 Tejas started experimenting with remote working. He and some colleagues set up remote work stations in Gandhinagar, Gujarat, India and their employers invested in reliable high-speed internet to make sure they could get done what they needed to. On his first day of remote working, he managed to complete five tasks that he described as 'successful in all aspects' (Patel et al, 2019). So far, so good for Tejas.

In a hospital in Ahmedabad, Gurjarat, 20 miles away from Tejas' remote workstation, a patient suffering from a heart condition called atherosclerosis was recovering from a surgical procedure known as percutaneous coronary intervention. The patient had had a stent fitted to open blood vessels in the heart that would otherwise struggle to function. Tejas was the surgeon who'd fitted it. Using his remote workstation and a CorPath GRX surgical robot, Patel was able to complete the relatively simple procedure without being in the same building – or even postcode – as his patient. If he could do the surgery from 20 miles away, theoretically, with a sufficiently stable and fast internet connection, he could have done it from anywhere.

When we think of remote work, it's easy to assume we're talking about doing from home something we've grown accustomed to doing from an office. There is so much more to it than that. Yes, people will find it easier to liberate themselves from the commute-to-cubicle pipeline and yes, people will recoup life-changing amounts of their own time from their employer, but – as we'll explore in this book – the switch to remote working has the potential to completely reconfigure the relationships between employers and their employees, businesses and their suppliers, businesses and their customers, and organizations and their local communities. Perhaps most importantly, though, remote working has the capacity to radically alter the relationship we each have with our work, our time, our families and our own selves.

But this massive shift in how we work won't be without risks and challenges. In June 2021, in response to how the global Covid-19 pandemic was threatening to disrupt how we work, the Tony Blair Institute for Global Change published a report entitled *Anywhere Jobs: Reshaping the geography of work* (Kakkad et al, 2021). In his foreword, Blair talked of a 'vast and profound change in the world of work'. The main thrust of the report was that remote work could do to white-collar workers what supply chain offshoring did to blue-collar workers; it specifically warned that without protective policy-making, jobs in sectors like media, tech and IT could seep out of the country to places where the cost of living is lower. The report didn't mention medicine or healthcare, but maybe it should have. Should heart surgeons in the UK be worried about the heart surgeon in India who can theoretically perform their jobs? Remote working isn't new and it isn't the sole preserve of desk-based knowledge economy workers.

On the same day Blair's report came out, the *Daily Mail* published an article with the entertainingly angry-sounding headline 'Get back to work! Furious bosses condemn Whitehall blueprint to give workers the right to work from home forever and make it ILLEGAL to force them back to the office' (Groves, 2021). The 'blueprint' cited in the article described how it could become government policy for flexible working, including working from home, to become the 'default'. A 'Whitehall source' – a name given to anonymous government spokespeople – was quoted as saying flexible working 'would cover things like reasonable requests by parents to start late so they can drop their kids at childcare. But in the case of office workers in particular it would also cover working from home – that would be the default right unless the employer could show good reason why someone should not' (Groves, 2021).

As we write this book in 2021, remote working is very much viewed as something we're doing because of the Covid-19 pandemic and the subsequent lockdowns. Many are still asking when we're going back to the old way of working and why we haven't already. By 2022, and steadily in the years that follow, hopefully we'll have stopped asking those questions and will view remote working very much as something we do because it's beneficial in a number of important ways. If in 2024 we're reflecting on 'that time when everyone worked remotely', society will have missed a massive opportunity.

This book will explore the methods by which we achieve a sustainable model for remote work that delivers on its promise. It will also explore the forces pushing against it, such as vested interests, cultural biases and affection for the status quo. The *Daily Mail* article mentioned earlier caused a minor stir, pitting business groups against employees and trade unions. The Trades Union Congress said any new rights to flexible working should only be turned down in 'exceptional circumstances', warning of an 'emerging class divide' between higher paid home workers and lower paid manual jobs that can't be done from home (Packard and Thomas, 2021). The Institute of Directors were not keen on the idea that the government could legislate for flexible working, saying: 'It is for the individual businesses to decide what is right for their staff' (Packard and Thomas, 2021).

While policy pundits were excitedly debating the nuances of 'flexible working', the matter became moot very quickly. The day after it came out, Downing Street rejected the contents of the *Mail*'s article entirely, denying that the government was drawing up any plans to make working from home the default. So where did the 'Whitehall source' get the idea that it was the government's plan that flexible working would become 'the default'?

Perhaps they'd read the Conservative Party's own 2019 re-election manifesto, published in November of that year, in which they promised to consult on just that, almost four months before the World

Health Organization (WHO) declared the novel coronavirus outbreak to be a global pandemic.

Proponents of remote and hybrid working must not get distracted and pulled into culture war squabbles. Flexible working was on the agenda before we even knew what Covid-19 was. What the pandemic did do, though, was enforce what the Tony Blair Institute for Global Change called 'a large-scale experiment in the ability to work remotely'. Most of us are still in the midst of that experiment.

Address not applicable

The rapid and unexpected shift to remote working has given organizations permission to do things differently. When American cryptocurrency exchange platform Coinbase announced their intention to go public in February 2021, they filed their S1 form, the official document required by the US Securities and Exchange Commission for any initial public offering (IPO), as required. Below the name of CEO Brian Armstrong and 'Coinbase Global, Inc' was a footnoted entry stating 'Address not applicable'. At the bottom of the page, the footnote read 'In May 2020, we became a remote-first company. Accordingly, we do not maintain a headquarters' (Samtani, 2021).

Of course, May 2020 was only a couple of months after the WHO's official declaration regarding the pandemic. So Coinbase were either extremely quick at pivoting to remote working across the board, or they'd already been doing it and had simply made it official when announcing their intent to go public. And they were not the only large organization to tell the world they were dispensing with the concept of a centralized office. In the same month the Chief Executive Officer of ecommerce platform Shopify, Toby Lutke, announced that his company was becoming 'digital by default' adding that 'office centricity is over' (Lutke, 2020).

As impressive and radical as such claims might sound, not having an office isn't a new thing. Lots of well-known businesses have been distributed, without a fuss, for years, including Sean's. We've been falling in and out of love with 'wfh', 'telecommuting', 'flexible working' – whatever we want to call it – for as long as we've had the tools to do it. And it's not been a smooth ride. It was an established practice as far back as 2013, when Yahoo! CEO Marissa Mayer banned it, insisting that the company couldn't function without all bums on office seats.

Shopify CEO Lutke is right, though. Office centricity is probably over. The genie is out of the bottle. What used to be seen as a perk for people working at tech startups has now been extended to people who work in banks, energy providers and insurance companies. They've become part of the experiment. People who may never have considered whether they actually wanted to work remotely, because it didn't feel like a plausible option, have had a taste. Employers may have been able to resist calls for flexible working indefinitely, had it not been for the Covid-19 pandemic. Office working is no longer the norm.

According to the UK's Office for National Statistics, the month before Coinbase decided to do away with having an HQ, just under half of employed people were working from home anyway. The vast majority of them were doing so because of the pandemic. Which naturally means they weren't working from home before the pandemic. So while it's easy for the CEO of an ecommerce platform to cheerfully dismiss the way in which a significant portion of people work as 'over', it's not going to be that simple.

Lots of things that used to be normal are over. Formal dress codes are over. Smoking at your desk is over. Fax machines are almost, but not quite, over. For a lot of people in the developed world, work being inherently dangerous is – thankfully – over. Since the Industrial Revolution, conditions for workers have been steadily improving; we put in fewer hours, and the hours we do put in are less back-breaking than our grandparents would have experienced. Sending a fax while smoking and wearing a suit, in the year 2022, would look weird. It didn't used to, though. It took years of lobbying, gradual changes to technology, the law, culture and politics for those things to shed their normality. Yet employers, unions, policy makers and workers are now being told the way they've been working, often for as long as they can remember, is over.

The end of office centricity is potentially great, in the same way that the end of an unhappy marriage is *potentially* great – there's the divorce to get through first. And divorces are messy and expensive. Especially if one party doesn't want it. And early signs suggest that many of the world's largest corporations don't want this particular divorce. The CEOs of Credit Suisse, Barclays and JPMorgan Chase & Co are all on record saying they want their workers back where they belong. They want to give things another go. They can change. Can we blame them? Think how much money they're spending on empty offices. You'd feel a bit put out too if your employees told you they were happier working at their kitchen table.

We're going through a huge and messy period of adjustment. Research conducted during the early stages of lockdown in 2020 indicated that some of us were handling the separation badly; adults were excessively drinking, eating junk food, playing video games and consuming questionable online video content during quarantine (Kelly, 2020). One half of the couple moved out and the other was sulking about it.

But there's a huge opportunity staring us in the face. It's a workplace accessibility revolution in the making. Disabled people, carers, people who don't want to live in a large city, people who just don't want to leave their home towns will no longer have to make enormous sacrifices to access the jobs previously only accessible to people happy with commuting or city living. Organizations will no longer be constrained by their physical locations. They'll save money on rent, cut their carbon footprint and they'll discover new efficiencies.

There are enormous social benefits to remote working, too. But we need to be careful. It will be dangerous to simply shift gear and accelerate into the 'new normal' without checking the rear-view mirror. What are we giving up, and at what cost? What, precisely, are we signing up for?

Increased productivity, more leisure, less traffic; these are all good things that potentially characterize the bright new future of remote work. The 'new normal', though, presents as many challenges as it does opportunities. It would be irresponsible for us to behave as if the world's previously on-site workers have simply been handed the gift of extra leisure time at no cost. That's not what will happen. The norms established in the coming years will be hard to undo. So it's essential to consider right now the entire spectrum of ethical, practical and cultural implications of employing people without necessarily providing them with a place to work:

- To what degree should employees accept surveillance activity in their home in return for not having to commute, for example?

- What privacy measures and other protections can be put in place now, so that working from home doesn't morph into 'living at work' in the future?

- Are we simply replacing one set of anxieties – the commute, office politics – with anxieties about burnout and children interrupting Zoom meetings?

- Will we become fixated on arranging our homes to make ourselves look more professional?

- Will obsessively curated bookshelves replace the expensively cut Italian suit as the de facto signifier of workplace status?

Balancing the obvious benefits – fewer commuting hours, more free time, a decentralization of talent and wealth – with the less explored drawbacks – lack of privacy, digital presenteeism and 'Zoom fatigue' – is key to ringing every possible ounce of potential from what has been, when accounted for fully, quite a disorienting and unpleasant experience for many people.

This isn't a book about the benefits of remote working and productivity. There are plenty of great books on that topic, and they were written a long time ago. This is a book about establishing healthy cultures in organizations that are adapting to remote working now, because of what's happened in the past two years. These may be organizations that are accelerating existing plans to pivot from office-first to remote work, or they may be organizations that had no intention of going remote, but who have since seen the benefits. There may even be a few organizations that aren't actually sure they want to be remote businesses, but have no idea how to tell their people to come back into the office. This book is for them too.

In this book, we'll explore the risks and opportunities presented by what has been an unprecedented shift in where, how and even why we work.

01

The new normal

To understand, define and promote healthy remote work culture, it helps to agree on a rough definition of 'work culture'. Unhelpfully, there isn't an overarching definition that satisfies everyone. It is a topic a lot of people and institutions already disagree on. Organizational theorist Elliott Jaques first introduced the phrase 'organizational culture' in his book *The Changing Culture of a Factory* (Jaques, 1951). Jaques summarized the scope of his research neatly, saying 'the part played in productivity by social and psychological factors has become particularly obvious'. The book was based on research he conducted at a metal bearings factory in London. But his observations could – with some notable omissions such as the importance of equality, diversity and wellbeing – equally be applied to today's offices and workspaces; the sanctioning of authority, analysis of change, the executive system and how these were affected and informed by social and psychological factors were three areas he explored in detail.

Workplaces were different when Jaques visited the Glacier Metal Company to do his research; for example, the book mentions women once, and that was to credit two of his own research fellows. Even so, Jaques' research noted that the factory was a relatively progressive place, describing the absence of unionization not necessarily as a shortcoming, but as an example of its 'advanced and novel methods', adding that 'it presented an uncommon opportunity to investigate how far a firm which had developed social practices of a more advanced character than was yet usual in British industry could nevertheless maintain satisfactory connections the larger social units of which forms a part both on the employer and the worker side'. His observations laid the foundations for what we now accept as 'organizational culture'. Institutions and organizations have subsequently built on what Jaques set out as his understanding of it. Today's competing definitions of workplace culture assert variously that it is based on shared assumptions, behavioural norms and collective values, but there's never been a unifying theory.

While most definitions of workplace or organizational culture vary on what culture actually is, they all tend to agree that the merits of culture should be analysed in direct relation to the productivity it confers. In other words, a culture that doesn't foster high productivity is a bad culture. Boiled down, workplace culture is what helps workers understand how to behave and how to work and what helps organizations get the best out of their people. Behaviours and styles of work vary from place to place in the same way productivity varies from place to place. Israel's working week starts on a Sunday, to accommodate Shabbat. In France, it has long been illegal for employees to eat lunch at their desk and this law was only relaxed temporarily due to Covid-19 restrictions on restaurants. In Japan, a country that has its own word for 'death from overwork' – *karoshi* – workers only take just over half of their annual leave entitlement, for fear of appearing lazy. To an extent, work culture reflects local culture. But should organizational culture be evaluated solely in terms of how it relates to output? We don't think so.

In the west at least, work culture has grown to address matters relating to wellbeing, absenteeism, employee retention, physical environment and recruitment. According to many recent definitions, workplace culture has become intrinsically related to place. Employers have spent vast sums making workplaces aesthetically rewarding, comfortable places that encourage employees to work longer hours and resist the urge to move on. Without an office or a factory in which to nurture a culture, can a workplace culture even exist?

What themes will most define remote work culture to begin with?

'The new normal' is a phrase we probably shouldn't be using just yet. What we're experiencing at the time of writing is an experiment, and the culture of remote working is yet to be fully established. Organizations, policy makers and employees are trying to make the best of a situation that in most cases was thrust upon them. It's safe to say that in two or three years' time it will still feel something like an experiment. As of now, what constitutes a good remote work culture is messy and ill defined. It's new, but it's far from being normal. Hopefully this book will answer some of the pertinent questions of what 'normal' might look like in the near and medium term.

Looking at the remote working landscape as it is today, normal varies by team, department, organization, region and country. There appear to be only a few common themes that characterize what we're collectively experiencing: an increased reliance on video and its associated quirks, and our anxieties about them; an emphasis on written communication; an absence of physical interaction; and an increase in professional and personal autonomy. Let's explore some of these unifying factors in more detail.

Video

'Lisa's Wedding', episode 19, season six of *The Simpsons*, was one of the many episodes to offer a depiction of the near future that turned out to be impressively plausible. It was first aired on Fox in 1995, predicting life 15 years in the future. In writer Greg Daniels' imagined 2010 America, air pollution had turned the night sky red, people communicated via wristwatches and video screens had replaced telephones. And while the writers were around five years too early with their prediction for smartwatches (the Apple Watch came out in 2015), they called everything else correctly. The scene where Marge and Lisa participate in an awkward, glitchy video call was something to which most people could have related by as early as 2010

As Lisa was preparing to get married in *The Simpsons*' fictional 2010, in the real 2010 America Microsoft was preparing to acquire a Swedish video-calling platform, Skype, and software engineer Eric Yuan was getting ready to leave his role as Cisco's Corporate Vice President to launch his own company – Zoom Video Communications.

A decade later, Zoom became an unmistakable part of our workplace cultural fabric. In 2021 it was valued at around $108 billion. Meanwhile, Skype For Business was being shut down. In the space of about three years, Zoom gained ground on Microsoft's 10-year Skype head-start to become the virtual meeting room of choice for remote workers. And in doing so it achieved something extremely rare. It replaced Skype not only as a product, but as the informal catch-all term for video calling. We still FedEx our packages, Photoshop our images and Google everything else. But Skyping your colleagues just sounds quaint. Forty million people a day were still using Skype as of March 2020. But Skype's quality issues, and the fact that Microsoft had announced its plan to discontinue the business version in 2021 to focus on its Teams platform, meant that Zoom could steal Skype's thunder at the very moment in history when the majority of the world's online population would have been absolutely primed to pick a video calling platform that would see them through the rest of their professional lives.

The story of Zoom knocking Skype off its perch is remarkable. If someone had asked you in March 2019 if you knew 'how to add a Zoom background', or if you had 'Zoom fatigue', there is a close to zero probability you'd have known the answer, let alone what they were talking about. If they'd asked you the same questions in March 2020, you still might not have known the answer, but there's a good chance you'd have at least known what they were talking about.

For almost a decade, Zoom remained a relatively obscure pretender to Skype's crown. Prior to March 2018, Google's index of 130 trillion web pages had just two pages containing the phrase 'how to add a Zoom background'. Zoom was anything but a household name. Now it's far more than a household name. Video conferencing is the defining feature of the remote work revolution. There's lots to explore about video conferencing later in the book, but it's worth us stating up front that not all of it is positive. We'd have struggled without it, but the platform of choice for remote workplace communications has already become a source of anxiety, resentment and paranoia.

More writing, less speaking

Organizational communication theory is taking an unavoidable hit during the remote working adjustment phase. It's not a surprise. The way we communicate inside and outside of organizations has been knocked completely out of balance. As workers and employers, we are still coming to terms with having lost a very important means of communication – face-to-face conversations. These face-to-face inter-actions can take almost infinite forms: hellos in the lift, informal catch-ups around the desk, daily stand-ups, in-depth appraisals in the boardroom, you get the picture. These are just a few of the missing conversational settings that spring to mind when we contemplate what we're not doing anymore.

As significant and important as these interactions are, it's not useful to spend too much time or energy mourning their loss. We can't replace face-to-face interaction. So what's the point of focusing on how important it was? Physical, face-to-face interactions and remote working are mutually exclusive. There's no getting around it. So it's far more useful instead to look at how we retain the benefits they conferred, without necessarily being able to directly approxi-mate everything else about them. Then we should be exploring ways to improve how we communicate at work using the tools at our disposal.

Video calling is doing a reasonable job of filling the gap left by structured meetings, one-to-ones and stand-ups. But for the casual, over-the-desk chit chat that we're also not having, video is not a particularly useful platform. For a start, all parties need to be willing, available and have access to the right platform. Then there's the effort of scheduling. When it comes to informal, unstructured and unplanned communication, the sort we'd have in corridors, by the coffee machine or on our way out to lunch, we're relying more heavily on the written word. Where you'd once grab a colleague for a quick question, you're now more likely to 'Slack' them than you are to speak to them. In fact, as well as replacing informal conversations, Slack and similar tools with built-in instant message functions are replacing email for less formal conversations, messages that need a quick reply, feedback, reassurance and gossip.

The emphasis on writing over talking means extroverts whose reputations were based on their personality and rapport-building skills have lost a means of demonstrating their personal value. And this is no trivial thing. People thrive at work for different reasons. One big reason people get on at work is that they get on with people and are nice to be around. Remote working takes away an important platform on which people have performed their 'at work' character.

Take Ross, for example. Ross works for one of the UK's largest energy providers as an auditor with a focus on regulatory compliance. Sean has worked with Ross in the past and can vouch for him. He is great company at work. Since the switch to remote working, he's joined a new team. We interviewed a lot of people about how they were experiencing remote work and Ross' insights on this particular issue opened our minds to the hidden challenges.

'From a personal perspective, I've always felt that I was a good person to work with and be around in the office space, and I have worried a bit that since joining my new team I've not been able to present that effectively.' Ross is a classic example of an extrovert for whom the workplace serves both as a place to get work done and as an environment to demonstrate his unique value. Being a good person to be around is a major asset, both to the individual, their colleagues and the organization. You can't measure it, but every manager will know which people in their team have the personal qualities that transcend their job specification and who simply make the workplace better. These are the sorts of people you want around you on your first day, or when you're having a rough time, or when you need some unsolicited positive feedback, a funny story or some gossip. These personalities obviously still exist, but remoteness has dulled their effect on those around them. Good managers will find a way to help the workplace extroverts shine through. Bad ones will pretend it isn't happening or doesn't matter.

'I think one of the biggest challenges of working from home has simply been not being able to quickly refer to my colleagues if I have a question,' says Ross. 'It has been a challenge. In the past, if I had an issue I could just quickly grab one of my team and have a discussion, but since working from home was implemented that's not been possible.'

Ross has taken action to recoup some of his lost influence. 'I have scheduled regular catch-ups with individuals in the team where we talk about things away from work and I have tried to generate a bit of the "personal interaction" stuff by setting up a couple of WhatsApp groups within the team so we can have a gossip.

'Working from home is fine for doing the work, but I do miss the general hubbub of being in the office,' he says. And he's obviously not alone in that. 'I've picked up any number of things from eavesdropping in on conversations and involving myself in the office gossip. That said, I'd certainly miss the quiet of working from home. In the office, you are working in a fairly busy environment and I do find it difficult to focus fully. At home, I can close the door and I have a distraction-free environment that I'd simply never be able to achieve at the office.'

There's a flipside to all this. For people who are a bit more reserved, the absence of the office as a performance space, combined with the emphasis on the written word over the spoken word, represents a fantastic opportunity for them to shine. Rachel, who we'll be hearing from in much more detail later, works within a large and complex government department. She describes herself as an introvert and sees remote working as a leveller.

'Working from home is great for accessibility and has the potential to put everyone, no matter grade, location, or ability, on a level playing field. It's great for introverts like me, too, because I can decide who sees me, when I want to talk, and I don't have to chat to people in kitchens.'

There will always be trade-offs. And Rachel has spotted a couple of very important drawbacks. 'I'm concerned that with less time together in person, workers will find it harder to share ideas, discuss pay and inequalities at work, and it could reverse progress. Who is going to be comfortable having sensitive conversations about things like that over Slack or Teams?' She's got a point.

The degree to which writing replaces speaking will vary by team, let alone organization, but being a good writer is likely to have significantly more impact on a person's career progression in a remote context than it might have had in an office context. And being an engaging, likeable extrovert is likely to have less impact, unless managers help their remote extroverts find new ways to add value. Writing skills aren't just useful for the interpersonal parts of our work. As we'll discuss later, remote working is going to bring about a major critical reappraisal of people's ability to communicate with clarity and precision over email, instant messages, in documents and via other channels too.

Back to Ross for a moment. His job isn't necessarily one we'd assume would transfer easily from the office to a remote setting. He works for a large, heavily regulated organization and he has to manage lots of moving parts. 'Essentially my job boils down to process management. I have to ensure that the processes used in the delivery of our Energy Company Obligation are easily understood by our subcontractors and that our processes do not inadvertently lead to my organization delivering non-compliant measures in respect of loft insulation, cavity wall insulation or boiler replacements, in the eyes of Ofgem, our regulator.

'There's also a certain amount of fraud investigation work that I undertake, and I write communications to our subcontractors whenever necessary, usually clarifying some part of Ofgem's guidance for the delivery of the Energy Company Obligation. I'm also the business continuity plan manager for my office, so I have responsibility for maintaining that plan, doing things like ensuring colleague contact details are kept up to date.'

For some organizations, especially those in tech and media, the switch to remote has been relatively straightforward because the majority of their core processes are cloud-based anyway. They were effectively remote working in the office. Toby Lutke's flippant but true claim that office centricity is over might grate because, of course, it's easy for him to say that and much harder for people like Ross who have experienced disorientating disruption to their work and careers.

And as we examine the ever-increasing list of reasons to go remote, we run the risk of biasing the experiences of organizations and industries for whom the switch to remote was nothing more than a natural progression of existing practices. We do this because they tell us a compelling story about how simple and liberating it is. It's important that we take notice of the people who are willing but struggling. The true value of remoteness will only become clear when we see how well it works for big, clunky, old organizations in heavily regulated sectors, like the energy company Ross works for. So it was quite surprising to hear that, from his inside perspective, the pivot to remote working was nothing more than a shove in the direction they were thinking of taking anyway.

'Initially I was quite surprised at the speed of the decision to impose working from home. We obviously knew that Covid-19 was on the way, but in all honesty I was expecting at least a week of discussions between key decision makers in the office I work in and the board before any decision to send us home was made. In terms of my personal response, I was more curious than anything. Working from home was something that I suspected would be implemented soon, regardless. The pandemic, in my view, just accelerated the process.'

This surprised us too, in a good way. But it's not a universal experience among people inside large organizations. In Rachel's experience, the organizational culture she experiences is not naturally cut out for remote work and, if anything, the gains she's experiencing in her working life are in spite of, not because of how well her employers are handling the change.

'Fundamentally, I think working from home as a real, consistent option is probably the greatest innovation during my newish career, but I don't think large, hierarchical organizations like the government are really set up to do it well. I do think there's a lot of mistrust from managers and it highlights, to me at least, how undemocratic our working culture is. We need a total overhaul of how we work, including the nine-to-five, and less reliance on old power structures and the cult of being busy.'

Ross sees lots of radical change in his future, too, but is more optimistic about his employer's capacity for delivering it. 'Looking at it from a business continuity perspective, I understood that what was happening would essentially mean a full rewrite of our existing office plan. Previously the plan could be summed up in one sentence: "If there's a problem at the office, work from home", but the urgency of the Covid-19 pandemic meant that this was effectively flipped on its head, with us now saying, "If there's an issue at home, come to work in the office."'

As Rachel says, trust is going to play a huge part in how successful organizations manage their migration to having distributed workforces. It'll also have a major influence on how well employees receive and adapt to those changes. It's already clear that, while Rachel is more sceptical of her employer's capacity to provide steady stewardship, Ross trusts his managers and has faith in the organizational culture to help him thrive.

'I think broadly things have gone better than expected. I've changed jobs since working from home so it's clearly not done my career prospects any damage. at least,' says Ross. 'Also, since Covid-19 related restrictions were lifted around construction last year, we've seen a massive increase in the amount of work coming through to us from our subcontractors. Being remote hasn't prevented us from managing this effectively.'

Ross' experience and those of his colleagues suggest that things have gone well and that decision makers have identified a sufficient number of positives at an organizational level that they're happy with the direction of travel, or at least not actively seeking to resist it.

'If anything, the success of the team has inspired the board and senior leadership to look at implementing working from home as a permanent "thing",' says Ross. 'I am aware that a working group has been set up to liaise with various teams in the business to ascertain the desire to keep remote working as an option. While nothing has been communicated, the general position seems to be that there's no desire to implement "five days a week at the office" anymore. I think those days are gone.

'If the result of all this is that we move to a hybrid model with two or three days in the office, the rest from home, then I would consider that a bit of a win and my feelings on it would be largely positive.

'As far as the future of remote working is concerned, my employer has set up a working group which is tasked with establishing what office attendance looks like moving forwards. The initial thoughts coming out of the group and my own conversations with colleagues are that they won't be imposing five days per week attendance in the office. This is important as they own leases on a number of buildings in the Midlands, so any decision around whether or not we return to the office will not be immediately forthcoming. Either way, I hope a decision is made soon as I'd quite like to get a dog, but I wouldn't do that if I'm required to work in the office for five days a week.'

Ross' hypothetical dog is a cute way to underscore an important point. The benefits of remote work aren't just about how we work. The issue is just as much about how we live outside of work. And the fact that he's even thinking about making such a major change to his life tells us that being remote is having a significant impact on how he sees his future panning out. Think of the same situation in reverse. Was Ross effectively denying himself a dog to keep his boss happy?

Remoteness from the physical workplace is going to have an enormous impact on people's professional and personal autonomy, their willingness to set new boundaries and their appetite for compromising on the things that matter to them outside of work. We're going to hear a lot more about this from people who have already started planning major life changes and improvements that they didn't realize they'd been denying themselves.

02

It's not just where we work, it's how we work

If you were born between 1980 and 1985, there's good news and bad news about your career trajectory. The bad news is that, according to people like author and digital teamwork expert Erica Dhawan, you're a 'geriatric millennial' (Dhawan, 2021). At time of writing, you are no older than 41 years of age and people are already calling you geriatric. That is objectively bad. You were born long enough ago to remember life before the ubiquity of the internet. You might be young enough to have spent most of your life using it, and the associated digital communications methods, but by millennial standards you are old.

The good news is – again, according to people like Dhawan – you are part of the cohort best suited to managing people under a distributed model. Your life experience, catching the tail-end of Gen X yet being a fully fledged grown-up by the time Gen Z entered the workforce, means you sit right in the sweet spot. Or, to put it bluntly, you've probably had a job where you had to use a telephone, but you've also got Slack on your smartphone.

And, according to Dhawan, the hybrid workforce of the future depends on the relatively rare blend of life skills already acquired by those who straddle the divide between digital and non-digital natives. In fact, the CEOs of Facebook, Canva, Reddit and Airbnb are part of this exact generational micro-cohort.

As Dhawan puts it, 'we've seen things. We're weathered internet veterans. We survived DailyBooth, Friendster, and Myspace friendship rankings, and yet here we are, feeling incredibly competent at the thought of creating a TikTok or a Clubhouse panel discussion' (Dhawan, 2021).

Remote working necessarily demands a shift in both culture and convention. We might be able to transpose some existing workplace norms into a remote context. In fact, some of the things we were already doing in the office are remote by design; when you're instant messaging on Slack, collaborating in Google Docs or managing tasks in Monday.com, physical proximity barely matters. For other parts of working life, we need a culture shift.

Career progress and performative productivity

One issue that is already confounding management teams is how to accurately measure the performance of remote workers. For some roles, the key performance indicators will simply transfer from the office context. But it is going to be particularly hard for managers of so-called 'knowledge workers', who are not measured on traditional units of output like sales or customer responses, to get a clear gauge on how their people are doing. That said, not being able to see their team may actually force those same managers to ask themselves an awkward question; were we ever accurately measuring their performance?

Accenture Strategy Principal Director, Russell Klosk, has long advocated for an analytical, data-driven approach to measuring the performance of knowledge workers. Klosk believes artificial intelligence can make performance analysis cheaper and potentially more accurate. For it to succeed, he believes that knowledge workers must be measured on what he calls 'direct and indirect productivity contributions' that vary by sector and function (Klosk, 2020). 'An accounting firm might measure accuracy and timeliness of reports and analysis with an emphasis on information sharing, while a high-tech company would measure not just the output of a DevOps professional in terms of lines of code but also how efficient the code is and how clean (e.g. free of bugs) the code is, as well as how well they promote social cohesion to help upskill the team' (Klosk, 2020). Klosk admits his approach may have limitations; it certainly wouldn't fully capture the various intangible benefits people like Rachel and Ross add to their organizations. But the data-driven approach does have the capacity to attenuate one of the more pervasive distortions of performance analysis. It's something we call 'performative productivity'.

Centralized workspaces and synchronous working hours foster unhealthy competition between workers. People strive to be seen to be going the extra mile, even if they're not doing anything but phoning it in. Sometimes literally. Workers may clock in an hour before their contracted hours or wait until their manager has gone home before leaving their desk, and that may be superficially attractive to an employer. But there is no guarantee those extra minutes either side of nine and five are adding value.

And there are so many ways to game the system. A 2016 study into 'competitive overtime' by a business analytics firm found that almost a third of employees deliberately sent emails outside of established office hours in order to appear busier than they really were. And a small percentage of those actually used email scheduling software, so they weren't even at their desk when those emails went out. Nicholas Henry, CEO of Xoomworks, the company that conducted the research, told *HR Magazine*: 'Being busy and doing long hours is not the same as being productive and effective'. The research also found that performative over-functioning made colleagues who didn't partake feel insecure. Henry explained, 'If people are having to stay late to complete their work there's something wrong either with their capability, productivity or workload. If they're staying late to impress colleagues and superiors there's something wrong with the culture' (Frith, 2016).

What we can learn from football

Nicholas Henry is right. There's a big difference between being busy and being productive. And there's an even bigger difference between being productive and being effective. Just ask the legendary Sir Alex

Ferguson, the joint most decorated manager in European football. Speaking about England striker Gary Lineker, Ferguson said, 'I have watched Gary Lineker never kick a ball in a game and still end up with two goals' (Bragg, 2011).

For anyone who had watched Lineker play, Sir Alex's remark makes total sense. Lineker was the archetypal 'lazy striker', apparently contributing very little to the game apart from those all-important goals. He broke a number of scoring records for club and country, but did so while carrying around a reputation as a lazy player. The irony of Lineker's reputation and that of similar players is that their perceived laziness is what makes them effective at their job. Why waste energy chasing lost causes when you can bide your time and wait for that one opportunity you can convert into a match-winning goal? But many football fans just can't get behind a player that doesn't seem to be giving his all to the team. That discontent can often influence perceptions from colleagues and management.

Former Manchester United and Bulgaria player Dimitar Berbatov has also been perceived as being lazy. Berbatov's critics accused him of drifting through games with no purpose. He saw it differently, explaining, 'when I have that time and space I have more time to think about where to put the ball' (BBC, 2020). His return of one goal every 2.4 games at the elite level of English football suggests he knew better than his critics. The same was true of German playmaker Mesut Ozil. Criticized during the 2017/18 season by former Liverpool captain Steven Gerrard on the basis that 'he just doesn't do enough, it's clear to see that, out of possession, he doesn't want to know', again Ozil's stats tell a different story. At the time Gerrard made his remarks, Ozil had not only created more chances than any of his Arsenal teammates, he'd created more chances than any player in the entire Premier League, languid running style notwithstanding.

For every 'lazy striker' who only merits credit when we analyse their stats, there's another, equally misleading player archetype; the 'all action, box-to-box midfielder'. Fans love them because they give the appearance of endeavour and commitment, setting standards for their teammates. And while there's something to be said for the infectious nature of hustle and bustle, outputs are what count. The over-promotion of graft and busyness doesn't just happen on the individual level. It can pervade entire organizations too. Analysis from the 2019/20 Premier League season found that the teams with players covering the most ground during a game were generally grouped near the bottom of the league. In fact, two of the three 'busiest' teams in that league season – Bournemouth and Norwich – were relegated. Or, as Sky Sports journalist Adam Smith put it, 'Relegation-threatened clubs putting shift in' (Smith, 2020).

Players running around a lot is a sign that their team is struggling to get or keep possession of the ball. We might say this is also true of employees who conspicuously burn lots of energy. Employees who are regularly in a state of intense busyness, working late and skipping lunch, are not necessarily in control of their own resources. And we rarely stop to ask what's gone wrong when we see someone behaving in this way.

Back to football. The player that covered the most ground in a single game in the 2019/20 season was Wolverhampton Wanderers midfielder Leander Dendoncker, who clocked up a not unimpressive 13.21 km over the 90 minutes. But this was an aberration in his averaged stats. Over the course of the season, he wasn't in the top 20 busiest players. He wasn't even the busiest player in his team over the season, with two teammates putting in more legwork over the long haul. So why was the Belgian so 'busy' in that game? His record-breaking spike in work rate was an outlier performance, most likely used as a tactic to neutralize the opposition. His lung-busting effort came against Brighton and Hove Albion, the season's busiest team. With both teams putting in so much effort, supporters could have expected a five-goal thriller with end-to-end action. Instead they got a dour, goalless game with a total of two shots on target and practically zero entertainment value. Being busy isn't the same as being useful.

Yet a lot of these busy players remain firm supporters' favourites nonetheless. For all their other qualities, Dendoncker (for example) also has impressive tackling stats and is positionally very astute, but supporters still love a player that runs around a lot. It's similar in offices. Visible signs of being busy are harder to miss than the signs of effectiveness. Some work cultures see being busy as a badge of honour. A rudimentary scan of the language on most jobs websites is enough of a clue. So employees respond by signalling how busy they are.

Who doesn't love a dedicated grafter who goes the extra mile? It's easy to see the early starter who eats lunch at their desk as a committed hard-worker without actually analysing their output. The appearance of productivity is often enough to convince. Yet favouring traditional, superficial markers of productivity of course penalizes the genuinely effective workers who get the job done without fuss.

When it comes to assessing effectiveness, managers can be cursed by their own biases. That's why sporting performance analysts have taken to working 'blind' and doing anything but watch the game as it unfolds. It's an approach pioneered by Billy Beane, the baseball manager famously portrayed by Brad Pitt in the film *Moneyball*, that's caught on in football. Proponents say it lets them analyse what matters, without being distracted by emotions or hard-to-shake biases

The distributed workforce model presents a similar opportunity. In concert with a rethink on traditional office hours, remote work culture can neutralize these biases to an extent, and allows workers of different styles to work without the anxiety of not *appearing* to be sufficiently busy. It's not about penalizing gregarious workers who like to show up and be noticed. It's about making sure the quietly effective ones don't go unnoticed. And data analysis is one tool that managers should make use of to effectively measure performance. For this approach to be effective, it'll take a large commitment from employers to dispense with the idea that busy equals effective.

Is it selfish to work from home?

Not everyone shares our optimism for the possibilities of distributed-as-default workforces. There are some strong arguments against it. In an article for *CityAM* published in June 2021, the Chief Executive of the Centre for Cities Andrew Carter argued that older workers planning not to return to the office when lockdown restrictions were lifted were 'selfish' (Carter, 2021). The thrust of his argument was that younger workers stand to lose out by being denied physical proximity to older and more experienced colleagues from whom they would otherwise be learning. He said: 'Pre-pandemic nearly everyone learned how to do their job by observing their more experienced colleagues in action. It was a form of osmosis – something that could only be done in the room, by listening to their conversations, picking up on their cues and watching them work day in and day out' (Carter, 2021).

Sir Alan Sugar is against working from home too. He stated in July 2021 via Twitter that workers had become complacent with the 'new style of working' (Sugar, 2021), argued that city-based workers should return to their offices to support the cafes and restaurants that have suffered due to their absence, and declared that he'd never employ workers who favoured working from home.

Unsurprisingly, some business owners with a stake in workers returning to offices agree with Lord Sugar. 'I think people need to be pushed to go back to work,' argued a London coffee shop owner who called into a debate on BBC Radio 5Live (2020). 'People are getting lazy,' he speculated, without providing much evidence. Speaking at around the time the UK government was relaxing some of its Covid-19 related travel and social restrictions (before tightening them again in the winter), the caller told host Nicky Campbell: 'We've had some city workers come back to work and the feeling we've got from them is that they don't want to be there,' before adding again that he thinks it's just idleness and a desire for an extra hour in bed keeping them away. He's so close to understanding.

Two out of the three points above made are fair; young workers do stand to miss out, and restaurants and cafes have suffered. He argued that workers should be pushed back into cities for the benefit of the small businesses that, like his, rely on their footfall. A robust response to his position might have highlighted the hypocrisy of calling home workers 'lazy' while demanding the government take measures to ensure customer footfall flows past your business's front door.

While fair, those two points are also open to being presented in a biased way. The Centre for Cities is a think-tank dedicated to improving the economies of the UK's largest cities and towns. Of course they want people back in offices. A study conducted by researchers at the University of Nottingham found that 'if everyone in the City of London worked from home that could work from home, they would lose around 70 per cent of their labour force. This works out at over £9 billion in annual earnings' (De Fraja et al, 2021). Of course the Chief Executive of the Centre for Cities is finding reasons to encourage people back into offices. He wouldn't be doing his job otherwise. And of course the caller to Radio 5Live who owns a coffee shop in the City of London thinks City workers should be getting back to their desks. There are lots of people with vested interests who see your choice to work from home as a major inconvenience.

Some of the arguments against remote working reveal a fundamental misunderstanding many have about the demand we have for more fulfilling lives. There's more to it than a simple desire not to catch a potentially deadly virus. The Covid-19 pandemic might have provided the jumping-off point for remote working, but the demand for more work–life integration far predates it. The public health emergency presented by Covid-19 forced businesses to do one of four things, depending on their capability and appetite for facilitating remote work: radically change how they work; accelerate plans they already had for changing how they work; expand existing remote work practices to more workers; or carry on pretty much as normal.

For an employee enjoying more leisure time, less stress and potentially even better productivity working from home, the correct response to accusations of laziness and selfishness is, quite frankly, 'Not my problem.' It sounds harsh because it is. But it's also true.

Since when was it the sole burden of more experienced employees to ensure younger workers could watch them in action and pick up their good habits? It's an obvious benefit of office working, absolutely, but it's the responsibility of management to find a way to fill the gap left by remote working. It's not incumbent on older workers to show up at the office simply because management doesn't have another plan for knowledge transfer, other than hoping the best practices of experienced employees rub off via osmosis onto younger workers. It is 100 per cent the responsibility of organizations and their management to find ways to bridge this gap. Established remote-first businesses have already found ways to ensure young workers learn the ropes, without demanding their presence in a centralized office.

And since when was it the responsibility of office workers to keep coffee shops and restaurants in business? Clearly, it's not. Some might argue there's an unspoken 'use it or lose it' agreement between commuters and the businesses that make working in business districts more pleasant, and that's reasonable, but as we'll find out in the next chapter, our consumption habits change along with our work habits and there's at least one coffee shop owner in the UK who benefited from lockdown. These businesses exist to make a profit from the physical presence of offices and office workers. There's no moral obligation either way.

There used to be similar resistance to relaxing workplace dress codes. Some people just didn't like the idea and would happily offer evidence-free assertions against it, citing discipline, productivity and outward appearances of professionalism as a reason to force people to wear expensive clothing that they found uncomfortable. There are still people writing articles in the year 2021 arguing why casual attire at work is bad, even though most measures of success would suggest otherwise. Workplace norms change, but there's always resistance. Remote working will be no different. People with vested interests will be arguing against it in 20 years from now. Let them.

Is it bad for your career to work from home?

As well as guilt-tripping experienced workers into going back to the office to help younger colleagues progress, influential voices were quick to pile pressure on young workers to do it for their own benefit. In July and August 2021 Chancellor of the Exchequer Rishi Sunak urged young workers to head back to the office at their earliest convenience or risk seeing their careers stall as a result of their self-imposed estrangement from potential mentors. In an interview with LinkedIn News, Sunak said, 'I doubt I would have had those strong relationships if I was doing my summer internship or my first bit of my career over Teams and Zoom. And that's why I think for young people in particular being able to physically be in an office is valuable' (Hatton, 2021). The fact that Sunak's current job literally comes with a house for him to work from shouldn't prevent us from considering his position. And the fact that his own civil servants appear reluctant to go back to their offices shouldn't either.

There's nothing wrong with his point per se; young people's careers might flourish more quickly and fully if they're surrounded by supportive senior peers. But he ignores some important caveats. First, not all workplaces are the supportive and nurturing environments Sunak says he was lucky enough to work in, so the young workers he's speaking to may be just as well off staying at home. And if offices are as nurturing and supportive as he claims, how does that explain the discrepancies in progress between workers who, up until the first quarter of 2020, were office-based by default anyway? There will always be a mix of what Sunak's friend and former Prime Minister David Cameron called 'strivers and skivers' in any workplace. Some people are desperate to accelerate their career progress and will find a way to make it happen, often by unsustainable overfunctioning. Others are happy just doing their work with no major aspirations of becoming CEO or desire to start clocking off any later than 5 pm. Both of these things are OK. Second, he's assuming that people are willing to put their career progression above the newfound lifestyle benefits of working remotely. While it may be true that, all things being equal, the mentorship on offer in an office environment will fast-track some workers up the career ladder, progress will come at the expense of improved career opportunities outside of that particular job.

The rise of the 'side hustle'

What do Apple, Instagram, Slack, Craigslist and Under Armour have in common? Aside from all being undisputed category leaders, they are all companies that started life as a side project by founders with full-time jobs (Love Money, 2020):

- Apple grew from a hobby that Steve Jobs and Steve Wozniak shared while working for other computer companies.
- Kevin Systrom learned to code and worked on an app called Burbn while maintaining a day job at travel tech startup Next Stop. Burbn later became Instagram.
- Slack, which we'll hear more about throughout this book, was developed as an in-house tool for collaboration.
- Craigslist and Under Armour both started life as hobbies that became profitable and then some.

The term 'side hustle' might be new (and quite annoying), but the concept has been around for years. In his 1926 book *The Richest Man in Babylon*, based on 4,000-year-old parables, George S Clason even alludes to the idea of having a profitable side gig: 'The more of wisdom we know, the more we may earn. The man who seeks to learn more of his craft shall be richly rewarded. Cultivate thy own powers, study and become wiser, become more skillful, and act as to respect thyself' (Clason, 1926).

As of 2021, at least £71 billion a year (4 per cent of the UK's GDP) comes from side jobs, according to research published in the *Telegraph* (Lytton, 2021). Estimates vary because definitions of 'side job' vary, but this is on the conservative side. A study by Australian outsourcing company Airtasker puts the figure much higher, at £346 billion (Cotton, 2021). Remote working naturally opens up a variety of opportunities for workers to develop rewarding and sometimes very profitable ventures while keeping their day jobs.

A 30-year-old digital marketing professional called Mona told the *Telegraph* that she used the 10 hours per week she recouped from not having to commute to earn more money on top of her existing job. She explained: 'I decided to use this time and looked into part-time, low-level marketing roles.' Fortunately for Mona, her cousin needed help with a new business venture and she was able to work an extra 5–15 hours per month (Lytton, 2021).

Some people have taken the concept of optimizing free time to pursue passion projects or bring in a bit of extra cash to unexpected extremes by using the extra time and privacy afforded to them by working outside of their office to maintain two full-time jobs. One such 'overemployed' worker called Isaac explained to the *Telegraph* that he'd earned £300,000 on top of his basic salary by 'double-jobbing'. His philosophy may not accord with the people employing him or the terms of his contract, but it's instructive nonetheless: 'just treat yourself like a business, start to think of it that way, as your Family Inc… if you don't prioritise your life someone else will prioritise it for you' (Lytton, 2021).

Setting aside the ethics and legalities of this extreme approach for a moment, the fact that since the switch to remote working an online community of 8,000 double-jobbers has established itself (Lytton, 2021) tells its own story about the amount of potential that's been sitting untapped in offices around the world. If so many people are able to work two full-time jobs without either employer noticing a drop in output, that puts an enormous dent in the argument that remote working hampers productivity.

On the less extreme end of the side hustle spectrum, remote working is already providing people with opportunities to expand their talents, develop entrepreneurial skills and generate extra wealth. And it's not necessarily detrimental to their employer that they do this. Sean recalls a former client that implemented an 80/20 policy for some of its staff. They were required, not encouraged or allowed, but expected to spend 20 per cent of their time working on projects outside of the scope of their employment. The thinking was that, by doing so, they'd learn and develop new skills that would benefit their employer.

Brian Dolan is founder and CEO of WorkReduce, a staffing agency for the media and marketing sectors. He's abundantly aware of the benefits of fostering an internal culture that supports employees who want to work on more than their job. 'We're trying to build the most diverse and talented workforce we can. If you're doing that, you will attract people who have other interests, and those can go commercial at any time. Why not embrace that, if you want people to be their best selves? Your career doesn't have to be your entire life' (Costa, 2021).

Employers probably should embrace it. According to research by the online marketplace Etsy, itself home to thousands of people with flourishing businesses developed on the side, nearly two-thirds of people with second incomes use office hours to do it (Lytton, 2021). And if employers can't already identify the ones that are doing it and definitively point to under-performance, they've already lost the argument.

Should you be punished for working from home?

The more people have adapted to life away from a centralized hub, the more outlandish the arguments against doing so are becoming. If telling people they were being selfish or putting their own career prospects in jeopardy clearly lacked sufficient punch to convince people to get back into the habit of commuting, stronger messaging has certainly been forthcoming. In August 2021 an unnamed senior UK government minister upped the ante, briefing the media on his/her thoughts on how we might coax people back into the office. The idea was quite simple; punish them.

Speaking to the *Daily Mail*, the minister suggested that people who'd found ways to be productive outside of their employer's premises were benefiting unfairly and therefore deserved to be penalized. 'People who have been working from home aren't paying their commuting costs so they have had a de facto pay rise, so that is unfair on those who are going into work,' they explained. 'If people aren't going into work, they don't deserve the terms and conditions they get if they are going into work' (Line, 2021).

How's that for a progressive industrial policy? Aside from being implausible – we don't know anyone who's been given a pay rise when they moved farther away from work – it points to deeply misplaced priorities. At the time this minister made these comments, the debate about which stick to use to beat people back into the office had been going on for about a year. If office working really is the best way to do it, where's the debate around making offices better places to be so people want to be in them? The entire conversation suffers from a failure of imagination. But then nothing dulls the imagination like a vested interest in commercial property.

Things got sillier in October 2021. First, Conservative politician and former Secretary of State for Work and Pensions Sir Iain Duncan Smith invoked Godwin's Law to get us back into the office; 'In the 1940s they kept coming to the office – even when Hitler's bombs were raining down' (Duncan Smith, 2021). On the same day that Iain Duncan Smith was fretting about high street chains suffering from lack of footfall and forgetting that the internet didn't exist in 1940 to enable people to work from home, some of his colleagues were blaming remote work for the resurgence of the Taliban. The unnamed 'senior cabinet ministers' claimed that the UK's 'work from home' culture in Whitehall left Brits at mercy of Taliban in Afghanistan and that 'key documents could not be shared with officials because they could only be viewed in the office. They included profiles of potential evacuees, read-outs of meetings and sensitive material about what was happening on the ground' (Mikhailova and Owen, 2021). If true, the tragic loss of life was not the result of the work from home culture, but of inefficient technology, or in other words bad office culture. If this was a PR campaign to get us to consider giving up remote work, it was a bad one. And it was being conducted at a time when Prime Minister Boris Johnson was working from Marbella, Spain. Offices for thee, but not for me, it seemed was the message coming from government, which was seen by many as a strange approach for the custodians of an economy that was suffering from a major skills and worker shortage. If anything, employment could be made more accessible by supporting people who want to do it but are unable to go into a workplace, for whatever legitimate reasons they have – children, caring responsibilities, disability, or a simple preference to not move house or commute.

The opposition to remote working isn't just political. It's cultural and it pervades organizations. Energy auditor Ross thinks he'd have had the option to work from home long before the pandemic had attitudes in his workplace been less negative. 'It always felt that working from home was inevitable. In my opinion the only reason my employer hadn't implemented it prior to the pandemic was because there was a group of "old school" senior leadership members who basically saw home-working as a skive. However, the team's performance over the last year has shown that office attendance isn't necessarily required.'

Why won't you come back to the office?

Let's pretend for a second that we achieve a global consensus on offices and we all accept that we need to spend at least some time in them to do our jobs. Then what? Do people happily hand back their lie-ins and extra leisure time in return for commuting and sitting in an open plan office again? Or do they start to resent their employer? Do they start looking at one of the many 100 per cent remote jobs being advertised nowadays. There's lots of them. Recruitment website Reed.co.uk reported in August 2021 that the number of totally remote roles advertised on its platform had increased by 452 per cent (Kochar, 2021).

Remote work is fast becoming a norm, but it is still perceived by many as a significant workplace benefit. Some employees will have been yearning for the chance to work from home for years before their employer was forced into letting them. Employers need to be wary about abruptly withdrawing it. There is a significant difference between not offering something your employees might want and taking away something they already value.

There are, of course, advantages to working in offices. And people already understand them, in the same way that people understand that there are advantages to cutting out alcohol and sugary food. It doesn't mean they intend to do it. What we gain from being in an office doesn't necessarily outweigh what we gain from remote work. And while we can replicate a lot of the ways in which offices are useful at home (or wherever), you can't replicate the ways in which working remotely is liberating in an office. A failure to appreciate the advantages of going to an office will not be the reason people don't want to do it.

Having to work from home during the pandemic may to some degree have helped people realize what they value about their office, but it has also – to a significantly greater degree – helped people understand what they dislike about working in an office and helped them realize how productive they can be outside of it.

Writing on LinkedIn about Apple's decision to insist its employees turn up to the office at least three days per week, the co-founder of a well-known Manchester media agency ventured his opinion that you can't please everyone when it comes to ways of working. It's an uncontroversial take. But, possibly by accident, this person also let their mask slip. Referencing the 'billions' organizations spend on creating workplaces that meet every need of their employees, he claimed that it's not unreasonable to expect the employees to show up. Actually, it is. And here's why.

First, as this person said, 'you can't please everyone'. Second, it's impossible to design an office that meets 'every need' in the very same way it's impossible to design a house or a car that meets every need. Striving to meet every need in any context is bad design. There's an emerging narrative among bosses and business owners that deserves to be challenged. It goes something like this: 'We've spent all this money – you're being ungrateful.' The media company co-founder writing on LinkedIn is no stranger to expensively appointed offices. His company's Manchester headquarters are very nice. They've got all the usual stuff that companies with 'great offices' have, including a very big slide, fake grass, hammocks, ball pit and ping pong tables. Not that this improves the working lives of his employees.

A 2016 YouGov study into worker satisfaction with their workplace environment conducted on behalf of the British Council for Offices and the estate agent Savills entitled *What Workers Want* found that the most in-demand features were comfort and control over temperature and lighting – three things most people can achieve at home but not at the office. A 2019 survey of 1,601 people at Harvard University found that workers want the basics done right. Study participants said they craved better air quality, access to natural light and 'the ability to personalize their workspace' (Meister, 2019), again, easily achieved at home, hard to do in an office. Both of these studies were obviously conducted before the Covid-19 pandemic shone the spotlight of attention on hygiene and ventilation.

There are lots of studies that ask employees what they want from their workplace, and most of them tell us the same thing. Workers want to be comfortable, with a degree of control over environmental factors like heat, light and noise, and freedom from distraction. We couldn't find a single study that told us employees want gimmicky toys or slogans on the wall. We're not trying to undermine the value of informality in the workplace – informal offices are great. But informality should be a function of comfort. And as long as bosses continue to publicly criticize workers for not wanting to return to the office, it's worth our while examining the fairly obvious problem. Employers don't seem to know what their people want from a workspace.

The media agency mentioned above employs a chief happiness officer. The job title might be yet another Silicon Valley affectation, but the role is real. We might expect that a company with one of these would understand better than anyone else what makes their people happy. But either they're not asking the right questions or, perhaps more plausibly, the employees don't feel comfortable giving honest answers, possibly through fear of seeming ungrateful. Because what the employees are getting and what the research is saying they want are quite far apart. There's overlap of course. 'Comfort' could mean 'hammock hanging above a ball pit', but it could also mean 'expensive but worthwhile ergonomic desk chair'. That's how we end up with confused bosses spending vast sums of money on things their employees don't want, but are too afraid to say, and why some of those bosses remain confounded to this day that their staff would rather work from home. We can blame the Silicon Valley tech giants like Google for this trend.

Culture vs environment

Duncan Riach is a writer and business coach. He happens to be very rich. He was a multimillionaire by the age of 27. Like a lot of rich people, he isn't sure exactly how rich he is because his wealth is tied up in things like stocks. He got rich working as a software engineer in Silicon Valley. As one of the first 'few dozen' (Riach, 2017) employees at a company making cutting edge microprocessor chips, he left what had been a lean startup at a stage where it had grown to employ thousands of people. The stock options he'd been given as part of his initial compensation package in lieu of a larger salary are what made him rich.

Duncan is by no means unique. Lots of people working in Silicon Valley become rich enough to retire before they're 30. And they don't need to be company founders or early stage investors to get there. Often they're just lucky enough to receive equity in a startup that goes huge. Offering equity is one way startups offset the risk to potential hires of joining a newly formed business. There's a risk it'll go bust and they'll need to find a new job. But it's possible that the company will become the next Uber and those early recruits who took a chance on a startup become very rich. This means that by the time these companies hit maturity they have a cohort of relatively young multimillionaire employees.

This gives these employers a problem. How do they retain these talented employees if they're already rich? A bigger salary or improved benefits wouldn't mean much to a multi-millionaire. And there's plenty to tempt them away – consultancy, non-executive board positions and retirement to name a few.

One way companies like Google and Facebook have tried to retain their star people is by creating workplaces that they love. By offering the sorts of workplace extras like gyms, masseurs, chefs, crèches and eye-catching offices, the hope is that these workers will not only remain loyal to their employer, but they'll want to spend more of their time at work, because being at work is so nice. Google's co-founder Larry Page reportedly insisted in the early days of the company that no employee be more than 200 ft away from food at any time. In its Zurich office, employees can use a giant slide to get to the cafeteria. And so the concept of the 'fun office' was born.

In around the early 2000s, smaller, less attractive and less cash-rich organizations attempted to approximate the 'fun office' aesthetic pioneered in Silicon Valley. They didn't have the cash like Google or

Uber to build genuinely beautiful offices. Some industries went over-board. It became something of a cliché in the media and advertising industries to see hammocks and football tables competing for floor space with printers and desks.

Before the Covid-19 pandemic – and during it too, by the way – job adverts routinely boasted about the presence of superficial quirks like this. In 2015 London creative agency Pearlfisher made headlines by turning part of its office into a giant adult ball pit. There were 81,000 balls. In 2017 a company in Salford did the same thing and got the same fawning headlines. The respective bosses of both companies talked earnestly about the perceived benefits of turning their workplaces into giant ball pits. 'The idea was to create an inter-active installation that promotes the power of play,' said Pearlfisher's Karen Welman in an interview with *Fast Company* (Peters, 2015). 'Collectively we are a family and to do a great job you have to love what you do. What better way of showing your appreciation for your family than making people work out of the world's largest adult ball pit?' (Roue, 2017) said Lee McAteer, the boss behind the Salford ball pit, presumably with a straight face.

We're not criticizing businesses that have nice offices. It's worth repeating: aesthetics and comfort are important. Employees benefit from having things like high-quality furniture, plant life and natural light. But despite what these 'fun bosses' might think, quirky add-ons are not culture. Organizations have long conflated culture and envi-ronment, overlooking simple but meaningful ways of improving worker wellbeing in favour of gimmicky quirks that look good on Instagram. The worst part about the fun office trend is that there's scant evidence to suggest it actually boosts morale or improves well-being. In fact, some employees actively dislike the infantilizing nature of what are effectively toys and gimmicks. A 2017 study conducted by London office relocation firm Kiwi Movers found that a quarter of employees working in so-called 'fun offices' found the presence of things like hammocks, pool tables and arcade games 'annoying'. The vast majority of employees polled said that fun office perks were of no value to them. So why was a removals firm conducting research into employees' office satisfaction? The CEO wrote in a company blog post that they'd noticed a lot of companies putting their football tables and hammocks into storage, even when moving to larger offices, which prompted them to look into it further.

Perks from home

Now that employees have got a taste for remote work, employers have two problems. First, if people aren't going into their offices, the hammock and beer fridge are no longer perks they can use. And second, for those who do return to the office, the presence of office toys is no longer benevolent. Anything that takes up unnecessary space in an office at the cost of distancing between workstations post Covid-19 will have a hard time justifying its existence. Workplace perks that demand attendance at a centralized location in order for the worker to benefit are not fit for purpose in a post-pandemic world. So what do employers replace them with?

Upgraded broadband

One of the biggest complaints we heard during the early stages of the pandemic was about home broadband speeds. An architect working in Manchester told us that she had to get a bus into her office during the very early weeks of the first UK lockdown every time she needed to upload a CAD file (a file type common to her industry that tends to be fairly large). Her home broadband wasn't fast enough, and each time she'd tried to upload it from home, she'd failed. She couldn't do her job without uploading the file, so she had to risk her own health to get the file uploaded at the office.

Slow home broadband can be a barrier to productivity and inclusion for a lot of employees; whether the consequence is a glitchy Zoom call or an inability to upload essential documents, it's a problem employers need to take action on as a matter of course. Employees should not be expected to foot the bill for upgrading their own broadband package. One employee of a university who has worked entirely from home since March 2020 told us his employer rolled out a policy of ensuring every employee had access to minimum upload and download speeds. All people had to do was send in a screenshot of a speed test and a copy of their home broadband bill. The employer then provided a stipend to make up the difference between what they normally paid and what they'd need to pay with their current provider to achieve the minimum specifications. That's more like it.

No doubt as employers get used to supporting remote work, they'll find ways to streamline this process. Mobile home broadband kits require no installation, can be used outside of the home for employees who want to work from a coffee shop or library and the equipment can simply be returned and given to someone else if that employee leaves.

Sleep packages

One of the most overlooked areas of employee wellness is sleep. Organizations have invested billions in wellness initiatives in the past; healthy food on-site, gym memberships, desk massages, mental health support all being popular perks. But since sleep (hopefully) only happens outside of the office, organizations tend to see the amount and quality their employees get as none of their business, despite the fact that it massively affects productivity, concentration, mood and general health. One study estimated that fatigue-related productivity losses were worth $1,967 per employee, annually (Rosekind et al, 2010).

An easy way to invest in employees' sleep would be to provide them with a budget for a top quality mattress and bed linen, blackout curtains or blinds, plus a selection of accessories such as eye masks, white noise machines, or in fact whatever the employee thinks might help them get a better night's sleep, within reason. Compared to a gym membership over the course of an employee's tenure, sleep packages come in significantly cheaper and are likely to confer more benefits to health and effectiveness in the workplace. Sleep packages are also one of the few worker perks that genuinely benefit all employees equally, as well as their significant others.

True flexitime

There's telling people they can start any time between 8 and 10, and then there's genuine flexible working. The former is a gesture towards flexibility that requires very little from the employer other than tracking time to make sure the contracted hours are worked. The latter requires the employer to first suspend their belief in the relationship between time worked and productivity outputs, and second to place an exceptional amount of trust in their employee. Genuine flexible working assumes that the employee will go days, possibly weeks, without clocking their contracted hours. It also assumes that the same employee will experience bursts of intense effectiveness that will recoup any productivity lost during the low activity periods.

True flexible working isn't suitable for all contexts, of course. But, where applicable, employers who are willing to ditch hours as a performance metric and build a reliable framework for measuring performance are able to liberate their people from the soft tyranny of 'nine-to-five, Monday-to-Friday'.

Flexibility around hours doesn't just benefit employees. Engineering firm Arup piloted a scheme in 2019 that allowed their 6,000 workers to spread their contracted hours across the entire week, including weekends. They could effectively work whenever they wanted to, as long as they did their hours. They launched the scheme, called Work Unbound, fully in 2021. And they're already seeing the benefits. Will Poole is a senior manager at Arup and he's taken advantage of the scheme. He works every other weekend and uses the time recouped from weekdays to spend more time with his family. Speaking to the *Financial Times* about the scheme, Professor Lynda Gratton, an expert in management practice at London Business School, said:

'Most companies are currently overwhelmed by the choice of place [between home and the office]. Some are also realizing that the choice of time can also bring real benefits. There is a crucial choice to be made – when can we disconnect from others – for example, to perform tasks that require us to really focus. That is the next big issue around the redesign of work'(Jacobs, 2021). Workers want flexibility. And as with flexibility of location, if you offer flexibility of hours and then take it away bad things happen. Stitchfix, the online personal styling company, once had a relatively happy workforce made up of people working flexible hours from home. These were people who, according to a Buzzfeed exposé, valued being able to fit the job around other commitments. 'Stitch Fix has attracted employees who – because they have part-time jobs, stay home with kids, or have a disability – needed flexible, remote work' (O'Donovan, 2021). When Stitch Fix changed that policy and tried to contract workers to minimum hours within set windows of time, hundreds of them, almost a third of the stylists working for the company, quit. Employees suspected the changes to their working patterns, which they perceived as a hostile move from Stitch Fix, was designed to drive them out because their jobs had become automatable.

Remote working is not a silver bullet to fixing bad culture. Some offices are genuinely terrible places to work. Some are great places to work. Offices per se are neither inherently good nor bad as a concept. They are what we make of them. The vigour with which we enthuse about remote working is derived from the many new possibilities we might discover by untethering ourselves from having to work at a specific place for a specific amount of time. But we shouldn't delude ourselves about what is and is not possible. We might escape certain problems by leaving the office behind, but the stuff that makes work genuinely unpleasant – the bullying, harassment, poor leadership, lack of clear objectives and monotony – will always find a way to follow us if we let it.

03

Recruitment, onboarding and retention

In one sense, the idea of a globally distributed workforce blows the traditional recruitment model wide open. In a world where organizations insist on centralizing their workforce in a single location, the talent pool to which they have access is necessarily constrained by one of two things: the likely length of the commute; or, if they are casting their net further afield, the desirability and practicality of relocation. Their ability to attract the best talent depends in a large part on local transport infrastructure and the appeal of the town or city in which they are based. That's even before we consider salary, job specification and the general appeal of the organization.

Distributed working changes this completely. Chris Herd, CEO of First Base, a company providing remote infrastructure for global teams, puts it best when he says an 'office first' model enables an organization to hire the best person in a 30-mile radius, while a remote first model enables an organization to 'hire the best person in the world' (Herd, 2021). That theory presents its own challenges, too. While your company may be able to cast its recruitment net globally, you'll also be competing with every other company in the world that's cottoned on to the opportunity.

Of course, the distance a person is typically prepared to travel for work depends a lot on what the job is. Retail and hospitality workers travel the shortest distances to their jobs and for good reason. These jobs are attractive in large part because they are local. It's a defining characteristic. They can't be done remotely (yet) and location has never been a barrier to access to this type of work because most people already live within walking distance of a pub or a shop.

When a role can be done remotely, there's absolutely no reason at all for organizations to focus on recruiting someone who just happens to live within a commutable distance, or is prepared to move nearer to the office. This is good. Not everyone wants to live in a big city or even move away from their home town. It can be a huge sacrifice to leave behind family and familiar support networks. Some people do it reluctantly because their skills are only in demand in certain parts of the world.

Amy Williams manages a large team as a digital commissioning executive at BBC Factual. She says being plunged unprepared into remote work was a challenge for her team. 'At the beginning of the first lockdown my team were super motivated. They were amazing, adaptable and committed to making it work. We made a lot of content outside of our remit. We threw ourselves into the work. We had lots of virtual social events, it was great. But as time went on, especially with this being a young team, motivation started to drop and creativity started to wane. People were going as far as questioning their career choices. To their credit they were open about their mental health issues. But the simple fact was that the team were missing each other.'

Recruitment

Like many, Amy's team managed to get through the disruption of unplanned remote collaboration using a combination of video calling, instant messaging, shared documents and a lot of patience. And now the shift to what the BBC calls 'hybrid working' is surfacing new opportunities for talent acquisition.

'I've already hired people who live miles away. Talent exists everywhere outside of the big hubs where big organizations exist. I've been able to give opportunities to people who – due to things like not being able to afford to relocate – may not have been able to take advantage of them before,' explains Williams.

In his book *The Road to Somewhere: The populist revolt and the future of politics*, journalist David Goodhart argues that there are essentially two types of people – 'anywheres' and 'somewheres' – between whom there is a cultural faultline (Goodhart, 2017). The 'anywheres' have what Goodhart describes as portable, 'achieved' identities, based on educational and career success, which make them generally comfortable and confident with new places and people (Goodhart, 2017). These are the people for whom relocating for career purposes is an exciting call-to-adventure rather than a potentially traumatic disruption. Goodhart describes the 'somewheres' as 'more rooted' with 'ascribed' identities. Goodhart estimates that somewheres represent about half of the population and the anywheres about 25 per cent. The other 25 per cent is made up of people who don't fit into either category. They're most likely the ones who don't want to relocate for work but do it anyway.

There's a tempting sociopolitical subplot to Goodhart's hypothesis; the anywheres flock to large, liberal, metropolitan areas with the most glamorous and prestigious jobs. The somewheres stay put, filling the jobs that are available to them. Decades ago they'd have been working in the jobs that actually played a part in defining their sense of ascribed identity – dockers, steel workers, the car industry, farming and other 'blue collar' work – but, as Goodhart argues, globalization has put an end to that. There's a downstream effect to this. It's possible that being one of Goodhart's somewheres limits your choice of career quite early on in life. Why would someone, regardless of their potential, dream of working for the BBC, or more generally in the media, publishing or national politics, unless they were prepared to leave their home area, or they already lived in London or New York City? Goodhart believes that the chasm between somewheres and anywheres explains why a significant portion of the UK population were so shocked when their fellow citizens voted to leave the European Union.

The *Anywhere Jobs* report from The Tony Blair Institute for Global Change (Kakkad et al, 2021) came to similar conclusions as Goodhart, albeit via a different path. The report's authors argue that the 'experiment' we've all been a part of has 'begun to loosen the binds that previously tied a job to a specific geography. Now, there is a new class consisting of relatively well-paid, professional white-collar jobs that can be done remotely anywhere in the UK or, indeed, in the world.'

Even when you control for the presence of somewheres and anywheres all around the world – it's not just a UK phenomenon – other constraints come into play. Regardless of your desire to relocate, the words on your passport can render you a somewhere when you want to be an anywhere. As of 2021, a German passport holder has visa-free access to 100 countries, while a Vietnamese passport holder has visa-free access to just 11 countries. All other things being equal, a German software designer is more likely to end up working for Google than her Vietnamese equivalent. Some people, through sheer dumb luck, simply have fewer barriers to accessing the jobs they want.

Yet Vietnam is thriving. In 2020, its GDP growth outstripped both China and the United States (Massmann, 2021). Dr Oliver Massmann is a Vietnam-based financial auditor and expert on the Vietnamese economy. He puts this growth down to the country's exceptional performance in the 'digital economy'. Hao Tran, founder of Vietcetera, a Ho Chi Minh City media firm, agrees: 'I think Vietnamese people are quite accustomed to working remotely… The monthly wages here are significantly lower than in the West. So Vietnamese people, who have skills that are relevant to being location independent, can actually earn a lot more money working remotely for clients overseas, or even companies in Vietnam, rather than getting a day-to-day office job in Vietnam' (Wilson, 2020).

Lack of physical access to high-demand job markets isn't necessarily a barrier to economic advancement. In fact, it fosters conditions that – ironically – are now ideally suited to the remote first future we're heading into. The Israeli freelancer marketplace Fiverr is a good case in point. It's a global marketplace in theory, but citizens of Pakistan, who with visa-free access to just seven countries have less international mobility than citizens of Vietnam, are massively over-represented on the supply side. According to a large-scale analysis of Fiverr's marketplace characteristics, 9.27 per cent of all jobs on Fiverr were carried out by someone living in Pakistan (Kalyan Maity et al, 2016), despite most of the orders coming from the United States and

70 per cent of orders coming from English-speaking countries; as well as the United States, it included the United Kingdom, Canada, Australia and New Zealand (Dean, 2021). Having their international mobility curtailed didn't stop those Pakistani designers, coders and search engine optimizers from finding the work that suits their skills. They just had to do it freelance.

Remote working has the potential to remove these barriers for those that want them removed. Remote gig economy freelancers may find themselves being brought in-house by organizations no longer limited in their geographical recruitment scope. Remote working also has the potential to kill the idea that aspirant workers need to 'get on their bike' – as former UK Secretary of State Norman Tebbit is regularly misquoted as saying – to go chasing the cool jobs.

Workforce distribution provides new opportunities for acquiring talent and new opportunities for accessing jobs. However, it also provides opportunities for exploiting the people with talent. And if organizations aren't alive to these risks, the recruitment process is where 'remote first' falls down.

There already exist a number of artificial intelligence tools designed to speed up the recruitment process. Some of these tools really came into their own during the first few months of 2020, when candidates were primarily having to interview for jobs remotely, by video call. A study conducted by the German public service broadcaster Bayerischer Rundfunk (2020) found that one AI tool apparently designed to speed up recruitment and make it more objective was itself biased and had the potential to discriminate against candidates. And it was the format of the video call that drew out those biases. The tool in question was advertised as being able to remove the human tendency to rely on stereotypes, making recruitment fairer and more effective. But the researchers found that simply altering the background of a candidate's screen significantly skewed the AI's perception of their competence. One example saw a candidate's conscientiousness score increase and his neuroticism score decrease with the simple addition of a fake bookshelf behind him.

The temptation to automate the recruitment process is strong. If it saves time (theoretically at least), removes bias and provides access to a global talent pool, why wouldn't you let a bot help you pick your next hire? In theory it's great. Yet this kind of hyper-rationalized recruitment process is only scalable in a remote context. And at scale, it erases or at least conceals a lot of the ways in which in-person interviews allow people to excel. Not everyone is comfortable on camera and many candidates express themselves better in person. The drive for efficiency and improved objectiveness shouldn't be at the expense of accountability. Otherwise recruiters are simply swapping one set of biases for a new set.

Recruitment can absolutely be done remotely. Telephone and Skype interviews are not exactly new and exclusive to the pandemic era, although they typically supplemented a face-to-face interview. It's do-able, but it's not easy. The entire culture of recruitment needs to change.

Interviews

The advantages of distributed teams that present themselves to a recruiter also apply to the human resources function. People who would have left their jobs because they wanted to live somewhere else can now keep their job. This is especially important when considering how many people moved to a certain city simply because it was where the work was. Remote working potentially relieves them of having to make the decision to quit their job in order to live somewhere they actually want to live.

It's already happening. In February 2021, music streaming giant Spotify announced its 'work from anywhere' programme, giving anyone who wanted it the opportunity to escape the sky high rents in the cities where it has offices, including London, New York, San Francisco and Stockholm. Spotify had clearly given their approach to remote work some serious thought. In order to help their employer better manage its own resources, employees had to commit to either working from home, co-working off-site or working on site for a year. They also needed managerial approval.

Spotify's announcement contained another interesting detail; employees vacating these expensive metropolitan areas would be keeping their expensive salaries. The knock-on effects of this approach, were it adopted widely, could be huge in terms of regional wealth rebalancing and regeneration. Not only does remote working have the potential to stop the 'brain drain' from small towns and rural areas to big cities within the same country, it could actually put it into reverse, sending highly skilled, highly paid remote workers with their impressive disposable incomes to places that would really benefit from their presence. It's not quite as easy for the same thing to happen across borders, yet. However, Vietnam has already proven that if people can't get to the jobs that exist elsewhere, they can create prosperity on their own doorstep.

At the end of 2019, Lancashire-based solicitor Frances was working for a law firm on the Isle of Man. She'd decided that she wanted to move back to England to continue practising law and had started making plans to find a new job closer to her family. 'I'd made the decision to move back to the UK and even though the legal systems on the Isle of Man and England are different, I was pretty confident about picking up where I left off because I'd got many years of experience in senior roles practising law in England under my belt already.' Although moving countries is never easy, Fran's planned move seemed pretty straightforward. All she needed to do was find a job, then work her notice period and arrange to move back.

'I was offered a job in England, so I handed in my notice in March 2020, just before the Covid-19 situation got really bad. As the situation was getting worse and worse by the day, I realized there was a risk I could be effectively trapped on the Isle of Man, unable to get to England to start my new job.' And since she'd handed in her notice, Frances took what turned out to be an enormous gamble with her career. 'I decided that I couldn't risk getting stuck indefinitely on the Isle of Man having quit my job there. It felt like I was in a movie. I knew I had to get off the island before it was locked down.

'So I left my job before the end of my official notice period. I'd tried to negotiate an earlier than agreed exit given the unique circumstances, but my employer was intent on me seeing out my notice period. So I felt I had no choice but to simply walk out, go back to my apartment and start packing. I was aware at the time that this might put me in breach of my employment contract, with all of the ramifications that has for things like references, but I genuinely felt like there was no other option. I made it back to Preston two days before the first lockdown was introduced, so if I'd waited to see out my notice period, I would have been stranded as I'd feared.'

What Frances didn't realize at this point was that her would-be next employers, like many other UK based businesses at the time, were re-evaluating their recruitment and hiring pipeline due to the economic uncertainty unfolding. 'The job that I had got lined up fell through. It was a shock at the time, but looking back I understand lots of people went through the same thing. So I was in a strange position of having to find a new job for the second time in a month when it felt like the economy was going into free-fall. I was lucky in that I had savings to live off and family to support me, but I wanted to get back into work as soon as possible.'

After moving in with her parents, Frances spent the next few months looking for opportunities, but the jobs landscape was totally different to the one she'd experienced only a few weeks before. In mid-2020 she decided to pause her job search and went to work at a Covid-19 testing facility. 'I wanted to be deliberate about the next step in my legal career, so I was reluctant to take just any job, but I also wanted to continue earning and I thought by working at a testing centre I might develop some new skills to take into my next role.'

The Covid-19 testing job was four days on then four days off, which gave her enough consecutive days to really focus on finding and applying for suitable roles on her days off. After a few months of finding little of interest, Frances applied with and was invited to interview for a firm in Lancashire, not far from where she was living with her parents. 'It was a remote video interview and it was the first time I'd ever done it,' she explained. 'It was fine. Although I came off the call fairly confident I wouldn't be getting the job. It was really hard to judge my own performance in that context because I had no real frame of reference.'

What Frances had thought was a fairly mediocre performance that generated little rapport, turned out to have been the opposite from where her interviewers were sitting. 'I thought, "There's no way I've got this job" after doing the interviews and carried on searching. But they offered me the job, which was a nice surprise.'

Frances' unexpected success tells a potentially valuable story to employers and hiring panels. Although she was performing well in the interview, she was clearly receiving feedback that she perceived to the contrary and by the end of the call was sufficiently resigned to having not done well enough that she continued her job search. For less confident candidates, the sense of 'this is going terribly' could be enough to derail or disrupt an interview in which they are actually doing just fine. Frances put it down to not being able to read body language and the general awkwardness of all parties being on video. 'I've actually done two remote interviews that have resulted in offers. In both cases, I believed I hadn't performed well enough in the interview to get the job and was happily proven wrong both times. I think it's hard to gauge how well you're performing in an interview when you're not in the same room as the interviewers and the interviewers are not in the same room as each other.'

Employers and hiring panels really need to consider ways in which they can give feedback to candidates in real time and explore ways to fill the gaps that are left by the absence of social cues, body language and the interactions between members of the hiring panel. Frances noted that in previous face-to-face interviews she'd done, she got confidence from seeing how her interviewers were interacting with one another.

Despite underestimating her own performance in at least two interviews, Frances' experience with remote interviews was generally positive. However, this wasn't down to anything her interviewers had done to help her. 'I've now done quite a few remote interviews. For the first few, I started off dressing formally, head to toe, including wearing smart shoes. Obviously nobody was going to see what shoes I was wearing but I wanted to do it because I thought this would make me "feel" more professional. I gave up on this approach the more I participated in remote interviews because I realized it had no real impact on how I felt. In the most recent interviews I've done I was literally sitting in slippers, jogging bottoms and a smart shirt.

There seems to be a correlation between me feeling comfortable and performing well in an interview.'

The most positive aspect to remote interviews, in Frances' opinion, is the total absence of peripheral stress and complications. 'I find travelling to interviews stressful in and of itself, without even accounting for the interview process,' she explains. 'Finding parking is stressful. I always seemed to turn up to interviews as a hot, sweaty mess. Remoteness has completely removed the previously "unavoidably horrible" bits of the interview process. It has completely changed my approach to being interviewed.'

This isn't to say remote interviews are necessarily free of peripheral stresses unrelated to the interview itself. As well as Frances, we interviewed a handful of other people who'd been through the process of remote recruitment and the most common complaint about remote-specific issues, aside from worries related to the interview itself, was the quality of the video call. One person we spoke to explained that her WiFi was fine but the manager interviewing her kept dropping off the call, leaving a junior colleague to continue the interview. 'As the interview continued,' she explained 'the other person kept getting pinged on WhatsApp with messages from her manager saying she was trying to get back in. There was one point where the girl was trying to ask me questions and trying to let her boss back into Zoom. It was really distracting but also, in a strange way, it put me at ease because I could see that the people interviewing me were having a hard time too.'

We can afford to be charitable about technical problems encountered during lockdown. Lots of companies were winging it and cobbling together an approach that got them through a very challenging period. But for organizations planning to recruit remotely long term, the quality and reliability of the platforms they choose will have a direct impact on the quality of the interviews they conduct.

Frances had no technical problems in her interviews, and got used to the dynamics of video, but she still encountered things that unsettled her. 'One interview I did that I found unusual involved being interviewed by peers, I presume to determine if I was a good cultural fit, before being formally tested and interrogated on my skills and experience. I found this particular interview a bit strange and did wonder if it was something that employer would have done had they been conducting face-to-face interviews.'

Onboarding and retention

After a relatively successful period of interviews, Frances accepted a senior in-house legal role at a financial services company. This was a relatively new experience, as for most of her career she'd worked for solicitors' firms. 'I started this job in the first week of January 2021. For the first three and a half days I was in the office. This was really useful for me as I got to meet the team and get a feel for the personalities and dynamics of the workplace.'

The firm Frances worked for had encouraged their employees back into the office and were keen to resume working in the ways they had prior to lockdown. They'd implemented all reasonable steps to keep their team safe and, at the time, Frances was grateful to start the onboarding process in person.

'And then there was a Covid-19 scare,' explains Frances. 'Because I was living with my parents at the time, I was really nervous about passing it on. I'd seen a few things in my first couple of days on the job that had made me uncomfortable, such as people sharing lifts to work when this was against government and company guidance. This made me unsure of how closely colleagues might have been following other guidelines. And because I hadn't had time to really get to know any of the people in the office, I didn't know who I could trust to be following the guidelines. I simply couldn't afford to give anyone the benefit of the doubt. So I wasn't comfortable coming into that office environment because I was living with my parents. So I asked to work from home.'

Her employer understood her fears and let her work from home. They implemented some tweaks to their working practices to help Frances get up to speed and feel included. 'I was really relieved that I wasn't risking the health of my parents for work. And I was grateful that they made accommodations for me. We had daily meetings every morning to check in with each other. I thought this was brilliant, a really nice way of keeping team morale high and helping myself and other remote workers feel included.'

Although grateful, Frances feels that without the first three and a half days in the office, she'd have struggled to build rapport in the same way she did. 'I don't think we'd have had the camaraderie we had on these calls had I not spent the first three and a half days working with the team face-to-face. When I was in the office, there were lots of easy conversations to have. We'd talk about what we'd brought in for lunch, what we'd watched on TV, and generally share some banter. There was easy access to topics of common ground. I remember feeling like I was doing a good job of fitting in. I must have cracked a decent enough joke because I got a good laugh from my colleagues and this really helped me feel like it sealed my place as part of the team. Without those first three and a half days, I don't think I'd have managed to establish anything close to the same level of connection with my colleagues purely remotely.'

Although things started well, she was only in this job for three and a half months before problems arose. Her employer had requested that she came back into the office full time, but Frances and her parents were not fully vaccinated and she was uncomfortable doing so. In addition to this, she felt like she'd got into the swing of remote working and saw her return as less necessary than she might have imagined.

Frances believed that she was doing really well working remotely and didn't want to disrupt the rhythm she'd got into. 'I think it was a matter of trust. They accommodated my original request to work from home because it was a health and safety issue for me. But when I queried the reasons why they needed me back in full time and whether it was justifiable considering me and members of my family were yet to be fully vaccinated, the conversation became a bit tense. I'm an experienced solicitor and I was expecting that they'd have enough trust in me to simply let me crack on with my work. But from their point of view, I was only one of two solicitors at the company.

The vast majority of their workforce were young and relatively inexperienced and the management had little experience managing more experienced workers.'

After three months, Frances and her employer agreed to part ways. Frances says they presented it as a culture fit problem and she's confident that she was more than capable of doing the work. And although disappointed, she now sees that role as an important stepping stone.

Having realized remote interviews were on the whole less stressful than in-person interviews, and having accepted that most jobs would, at least for what was the foreseeable future, be performed remotely, Frances was able to broaden her horizons, both geographically and in terms of the jobs and organizations she took an interest in. 'Because the cost and stress of physically going to interviews was taken away, I took a more of a scattergun approach to applying for work,' she explained. 'This included applying for jobs that I wouldn't have necessarily felt confident about applying for, because the worst that could happen was that I'd have spent an hour of my life on Zoom rather than enduring the stress of travelling to an office.

'The organization I work for now is an industry regulator based predominantly in Birmingham with a presence in London. I live in Lancashire and have no desire to relocate again so soon after moving back from the Isle of Man, so remote working has worked out well in that respect. I simply wouldn't have been able to get this job before the Covid-19 pandemic. Before remote working I would have had to move house or face an expensive five-hour round trip. This job simply wouldn't have been an option to me because there are no similar jobs to this where I live. I really, really enjoy this job and I only have to be in Birmingham once a month. Having passed the probation period well I can tell that they really appreciate me and what I bring to this role.'

Although she's happy in her role and likes the organization she works for, being offered the job as a remote worker has highlighted to Frances some of the apparent geographical barriers to advancement that had become prevalent in the UK jobs market, especially in competitive and prestigious sectors like law. 'There are people in this organization whose careers have benefited, in part, because they simply lived nearby and saw the organization as a viable option. That option wasn't available to me and wasn't available to anybody living outside of London or Birmingham. Remote working has made certain jobs in my profession more accessible, which is good, but it's a shame that inaccessibility was an issue at all. Organizations are now opening their doors to people from a greater geographical radius than their local postcode. Before remote working became a norm, I don't think these organizations would have considered hiring someone like me who could only make it into the office one day a month.'

She sees the positives of her own situation, but worries that her career may have been hampered by geography. 'Ironically, now that I've got a job I love with an organization based in the Midlands, this is the first time in my life I've felt disadvantaged by living up north. Before remote working, it simply wouldn't have occurred to me that I could have gone and worked for our industry's regulatory body. I had settled on the idea that I'd either need to move away or work for local firms. I'm meeting people now who have fallen into this particular career because this particular office was nearby, whereas I've slogged away in private practice, which is a very stressful and unforgiving environment, in order to get here. I wonder how many other people who could have done this job simply never considered coming to work here because it would have taken them away from their homes. It's positive that geography is becoming less of a constraint on career choice.'

Adapting to change

Frances' optimism tells its own story. In a few months and only through realizing she found she could adapt well to remote recruitment and remote work, she's contemplating how far she can run with the remote or hybrid model. 'It's not an impossibility that I could do this job from anywhere in the world if I wanted to. The idea that I could move to Barcelona or anywhere I like without necessarily giving up my job is very liberating. I don't know if I'd ever do it, but it's genuinely liberating to know that the option might be there. I like to travel and it's also good to know that if I wanted to travel I could still theoretically keep this job. That's never been an option before.'

And although she's happy in the role and feels like she's thriving, Frances did initially find a totally remote on-boarding process difficult. 'I found it a lot harder to build rapport with some people. People present themselves differently in a remote context. Some people exaggerate parts of their personality and other people down play parts of theirs. I would have been able to better grasp the office politics and characters in the organization sooner if I'd met them in person.'

It wasn't just interpersonal matters that left Frances feeling disorientated. 'I'd been told that one of my managers was really tall but obviously it's hard to tell over Zoom. I'd only seen this particular line manager from the neck upwards and without realizing it I'd built up a picture of their physical persona as being quite athletic and formidable. So I was really surprised when we met in person and they were, in the kindest possible way, a lot more pear-shaped than I'd imagined.'

Although it seems like quite a trivial thing, Frances isn't alone in having found meeting work colleagues in 'real life' strange after getting to know them remotely. Plenty of the people we interviewed for this book revealed that meeting people face-to-face for the first time after having worked with them for months was strange for them.

'I actually think this did affect my perceptions of them going forward,' says Frances. 'I think you base a lot of assumptions about competence on how someone physically comports themselves. It's quite disorientating when the physical reality of that person doesn't accord with the vision of them you'd built up in your own mind. This particular person seems significantly less confident in real life. This may be because they actually are less confident in real life – or more confident remotely – or it may be because I was perceiving a lack of confidence in real life because I'd misperceived them over video.'

Without physical, face-to-face interactions and all of the attendant subtle cues, body language and gestures, we're prone to making bad assumptions. Frances agrees. 'There was another colleague who was in the habit of turning his camera off during meetings due to having slow broadband. He spoke quite slowly and had a distinctive, deep voice with a very authoritative spoken demeanour. I'd built up an image of this person as being older, senior and very experienced.'

This colleague moved house during Frances' first few months in the job. His new house had more reliable WiFi, which meant he was able to join in with video calls. 'My perceptions of him couldn't have been more off the mark,' admits Frances. 'This older, avuncular personality I'd pieced together in my own mind was actually a man in his early twenties wearing a topknot and a goatee beard. This actually shocked me, but also it was a really handy reminder to myself about prejudging people based on quite a limited set of characteristics. That's part of the issue of working remotely. Had we been in the office together I wouldn't have the opportunity to concoct such an inaccurate picture of them.'

There are potential benefits for less confident or outgoing employees, though. Managers should be supportive of workers who want to retain a degree of physical privacy while working remotely. Different communication channels suit different people. For every person that thrives on a Zoom call, there could be two people internally cringing inside. Managers also must consider how physical privacy intersects with accessibility and equality. For some people, keeping a relatively low profile is what helps them overcome certain invisible workplace barriers.

Thinking about prejudging her 'faceless' colleague, Frances remembers a former boss who used her facelessness and her gender-neutral name to her advantage. 'The situation reminded me of my old boss, a woman called Rowan. She used to tell me she loved having an ambiguous first name because it made it harder for people to make assumptions about her before they met. She said it was disarming for people to have assumed she was a man to then meet her and find out she was a woman.'

From the perspective of a new starter going through the onboarding process, Frances' personal preference was for seeing everyone as much as possible, even if it was just via Zoom or Microsoft Teams. 'It's really helpful for people to have their cameras on for work meetings in order to approximate as much of the "real life" dynamic as possible,' she explains. 'Or at the very least, and this may be an unpopular opinion, let people know why they don't have their cameras on. During the early stages of this role, I was assuming that if people didn't have their cameras on it was because they didn't want to "properly" interact with me. I found it really helped me to get to know people by being able to pick up their social cues and I struggle to interact with people in the same way if I can't see their face or hands.'

There's another useful bit of feedback for employers here. Frances understood the benefits of seeing people's faces, but she also understood that not everyone wanted to do it. So she accepted that she would need to work around the lack of visual cues where necessary. But at least she was clear on what her employer's policy was. There are benefits and drawbacks to both. And we'll explore 'Zoom fatigue' in more detail in Chapter 9. The important thing is consistency and clarity; employees need to understand the ground rules and all changes need to be communicated with empathy. In Frances' previous job the reverse policy was in place to begin with. 'Everyone had their camera off for video meetings,' says Frances. 'But then the manager changed the policy and began to insist that we all had our cameras on. I felt that the way he communicated this change was harmful. It felt like a demand based on a lack of trust. And because the atmosphere was otherwise quite relaxed and friendly, it jarred a little bit and I felt like I was caught off-guard.'

As remoteness relates to knowledge transfer, training and skills, Frances appreciates the opportunity to learn in comfort. 'In a lot of ways learning remotely is easier,' she says. 'Because Microsoft Teams allows users to take control of each other's computers, you can structure training in a way that suits the recipient. If you're physically sharing a computer to do training, one person is sitting awkwardly peering over the other person's shoulder. Sharing screens remotely makes the learning process easier because it is physically more comfortable. You're not having to adjust your posture, squint at the screen or be mindful of the person's physical space. You can sit there for a long time, learning more and getting closer to where you want to be.'

She also believes that, while remoteness confers improvements for formal training, it takes away opportunities for the more informal types of knowledge transfer that would happen in an office environment. 'Informal learning is less accessible in the remote context because you're simply less likely to have off-the-cuff conversations about things like shortcuts and tricks. Because you don't have the chit-chat in between periods of formal training, you're only really likely to learn what's on the agenda and are significantly less likely to pick up knowledge in that off-the-cuff way that can be so valuable.'

In general terms, Frances sees remoteness as a net positive to her working life. She's been through a number of experiences – job hunting, recruitment, onboarding and exit – that give her a broad perspective on what remote working has to offer. 'I really enjoy having no morning commute. I like not having to dress in a certain way every day. I like the fact that the barriers between being at home and "at your desk" are not there any more. Although I understand that it takes discipline to maintain a distinction between working and not working. I like the fact that if I don't feel great for whatever reason, I can literally go and have a lie down without judgement.

But she also understands that we're still in something of an experiment. The concept of 'going to work' has been constant through most of her adult life and it's remained a relatively predictable experience constrained by location and time even as other parts of her life have changed. She has valid concerns about how remote working will interact with life changes she hasn't encountered yet. 'I am concerned that when I move out of my parents' home I'll be lonely, and that the connections I used to get from being in an office won't be there any more and I won't have that reason to leave the house every day that I had when I was office-based. This will especially be the case in winter when it's just harder to motivate yourself to get out of the house in general.'

04

Social impact

Remote working doesn't just affect how we go about doing our jobs. Its influence will extend beyond work, commerce and the economy and it will reach into our social fabric and pull at the threads that make up our communities too. As well as observing a 'vast and profound change in the world of work', Tony Blair cited the 'secondary effects on businesses that serve the conventional office' in the foreword to his institute's report on 'anywhere jobs'. Blair was referring to businesses within the direct gravitational pull of the traditional office – the dry cleaners and the sandwich shop that thrive because of their proximity to offices as well as businesses like cleaning companies and security companies who thrive because of their relationships with the office itself. The gravitational pull of a physical office is strong, but the impact of office closures reach much farther than the immediate vicinity.

Consulting firm McKinsey estimates that around 20 per cent of the workforce could soon be working from home at least three days a week (McKinsey, 2020). That means four times as many people will be working from home post-pandemic compared to before. It's not possible for that to happen without a profound effect on local and regional economies, transport and culture. There are positives to this, but it's not a simple case of neighbourhood coffee shops gaining in proportion to the degree by which city centre chains lose out.

'Even as offices decline,' proposes urban theorist and economist Richard Florida, 'the community or the neighbourhood or the city itself will take on more of the functions of an office' (Hoffower, 2021).

Florida, talking to Business Insider, added, 'People will gravitate to places where they can meet and interact with others outside of the home and outside of the office.'

As of September 2021, we haven't been in our remote working experiment long enough to understand or even hazard an educated guess at precisely how remote work will impact the fabric of towns and cities. The authors of McKinsey's study assert that broadly adopted remote work has always been an underlying possibility and that it was culture and to some degree technology that was constraining us: 'The virus has broken through cultural and technological barriers that prevented remote work in the past, setting in motion a structural shift in where work takes place, at least for some people.'

At least for some people. That brief qualifying phrase is very important. Some people will never be able to work remotely, from home or elsewhere. You can't deliver a pizza or care for a terminally ill cancer patient over Zoom. Remote work is severely biased towards people in the so-called 'knowledge economy'. Before the pandemic, knowledge workers may have been sufficiently distinct that they lacked a collective identity; you wouldn't necessarily lump in financial auditors with animators. Now they may all end up defined by the fact that they don't have to leave the house to do their job.

There's a non-trivial probability that this state of affairs will lead to resentment. And it's hard not to be sympathetic. Before the pandemic drove economies to rapidly adopt remote working, there was some sort of solidarity in the idea that no matter what you did for a job, you had to get off your backside to go and do it. Now, we're heading in a direction where there are two classes of workers; those that work where they like, and those that serve them. This friction was particularly jarring during the pandemic. The idea of a low-paid delivery driver risking their health so a highly-paid IT consultant could enjoy a gourmet burger in the afternoon is bleak.

It's absolutely essential, when considering the relative merits of remote work, the best paths to effectiveness and the mental health impact of remote workers, that we don't lose sight of the fact that we're really only talking about white collar, knowledge economy workers. Estimates vary wildly depending on geography and criteria, but more than half of the UK's workforce are employed in the knowledge economy. There are approximately 6 million private businesses in the UK in total, according to 2019 government data (Department for Business, Energy and Industrial Strategy, 2019) and approximately 2.5 million businesses operating in the knowledge economy, according to data published by NatWest Bank in 2019 (Waugh, 2019).

Not everyone can work remotely (and not everyone wants to)

When former Manchester United and England footballer Neil Webb was photographed working as a postman after he'd retired from a fairly high-profile career in football, the media reported it as a fall from grace deserving of pity. Webb's 'situation' made the front page of *The Sun*. The footballer didn't understand the fuss. And he certainly didn't see his job as a source of shame, greeting a reporter's feigned incredulity that he'd once played for England and was now happy delivering letters with 'What's wrong with that?' (Kimmage, 2004). Webb said he liked the fresh air and the walk kept him fit. Certain sections of white-collar society have the annoying habit of assuming that they know what's best for everyone else. In his 2020 book *The Coming of Neo-Feudalism: A warning to the global middle class*, Joel Kotkin explores and expands on philosopher-poet Samuel Taylor Coleridge's notion of the 'clerisy'. Coleridge believed that for a society to thrive, there should exist an intellectual elite via whom knowledge should be diffused to the rest of society. He called this elite the clerisy. The intelligentsia that existed in Tsarist Russia and parts of Eastern Europe are analogous to Coleridge's idea of the clerisy. Kotkin fears that we're fast heading toward a neo-feudal society where the 'knowledge class' assumes too much influence over classes it deems as inferior, arguing: 'Our new overlords do not wear chain mail or top hats, but instead direct our future in jeans and hoodies. These technocratic elites are the twenty-first-century realization of what Daniel Bell prophetically labeled "a new priesthood of power" based on scientific expertise.'

One of the risks we face as a society when wrangling with the benefits and drawbacks of remote working is overlooking the people who never worked in an office to begin with. Some jobs aren't calibrated for remote working and that's OK. It's more than OK actually. Not everyone is in their current job because they're trying to hit the peak of their intellectual capacity. Some people do what they do solely to pay the bills, to fund other interests or – and there's plenty of people who find this hard to believe – they enjoy doing things like delivering parcels in the fresh air.

The Covid-19 pandemic forced us to radically change our perceptions of jobs like shelf-stacking, order picking, dispensing and delivering. Or at least it should have. These jobs traditionally lack prestige because they are seen to involve relatively low-skill, high-effort tasks that can be taught relatively quickly. They also lack prestige, we think, because they don't 'require' a smart office. While white collar workers and economics pundits are debating the best blend of remote and office working, the workers we relied on the most heavily, the essential workers, are more likely to be wondering whether their roles will eventually be automated.

The uptake of remote working will vary significantly by geography. Some countries have a far higher proportion of 'knowledge economy' workers and industries that are amenable to remote working. McKinsey's remote working article, entitled 'What's next for remote work: An analysis of 2,000 tasks, 800 jobs, and nine countries', stated that 'the potential for time spent on remote work drops to 12 to 26 percent in the emerging economies we assessed. In India, for instance, the workforce could spend just 12 percent of the time working remotely without losing effectiveness.'

These variances will play out locally too. It's already happening as policy pundits and journalists speculate about the future of work. As is often sadly the case in the UK, London is treated as the 'default' UK city, despite it being a total outlier unlike any other UK city in terms of economy or demographics. This happens simply because many of the UK's most influential pundits live there and see the UK through the prism of their home town. And it leads to assumptions about what people want and need that can't necessarily be transposed to the rest of the UK.

For example, the assumption that the youngest knowledge economy workers mainly live in house-shares, making working from home unsuitable long term, seems to have become an accepted truth about young workers generally, when in reality it mainly applies to those in London and to a lesser extent to those living in other large cities. For London, it's true and it is indeed a problem. CityAM's Rachel Cunliffe examined London's work-from-home problem in fascinating detail, noting that, according to a study by London School of Economics and property developer Pocket Living, 'young Londoners living in shared properties – that is, the vast majority of the capital's young workforce – had on average 9.3 square metres of personal space to themselves during lockdown. For context, that's about the size of a small garage' (Cunliffe, 2020).

Cunliffe also pointed out that 37 per cent of Londoners in house shares worked and slept in their bedrooms during lockdown; a horrible state of affairs but one that is neither representative of the situation for people living in the rest of the UK, nor one that is likely to persist long term now that alternatives like co-working spaces and coffee shops are open again. London is not typical of the UK, New York City is not typical of the United States and Paris is not typical of France. But the experiences of people in those places could end up being used as a compelling – albeit unrepresentative – case for bringing workforces back into offices as quickly as possible. Global cities, and we can include Tokyo, Shanghai, Hong Kong, Beijing, Sydney, Toronto and Los Angeles alongside London, Paris and NYC in that definition, are necessarily characterized by two countervailing forces; high residential rents and a concentration of commercial real estate, with the latter often influencing the former. The outsized influence of these places on the culture and media of their wider geographical area makes it very easy to assume that all over the country young workers are sitting crammed inside expensive house-shares while perfectly nice offices, a walkable distance from said house-shares, sit empty. It's happening, of course, and it's not a healthy state of affairs for those suffering, but it's not happening in a degree proportionate to its media coverage. If you search Google.co.uk for 'working from home shared house', the top five results are from the London School of Economics, London Evening Standard, Loch Associates, *Guardian* and Stylist Magazine – all organizations that are based in London. In fact, perhaps ironically, the likes of Paris, New York and London are most likely to adapt quickest to hybrid working due to high office costs and an already embedded culture of remote working in the organizations that call those cities home, according to a 2021 report cited by *CityAM* (Willems, 2021).

We should feel bad for people who moved to large cities because of work who found themselves isolated and working from a kitchen table during lockdown. And although it's unlikely that those experiences will have persisted for too long after restrictions were eased, organizations do need processes and systems in place to identify people in such scenarios and support them. What we shouldn't do is use the plight of younger workers to discredit the many career and lifestyle benefits of remote work.

The stay-at-home commuter

Heaton Chapel railway station in Stockport, England, is the penultimate stop before Manchester's Piccadilly terminus for local passengers travelling north into the city. It's a pretty, two-platform station with a small ticket office, newsagent and planter boxes tended to by a group called Friends of Heaton Chapel Station. In 2019 the station served just under 800,000 passengers from the four nearby villages, making it one of the busiest suburban stations in the region. Just outside the station is a parade of former coal merchant huts that have been turned into independent retail units, one of which is B'Spoke Coffee, a speciality coffee house.

During the second UK Covid-19 lockdown, B'Spoke's co-owner Nick Harris said when we interviewed him that he'd experienced an increase in footfall, despite the vast majority of rail commuters – his customers – working from home. 'Lots of our regulars have made a point of coming by and getting a coffee during lockdown. Some did it because they wanted to support us and some did it because getting their coffee was an important part of their morning routine.

'But what surprised me was the amount of new customers we got. People were telling us they'd walked past our hut every day on the way to get the train, but never had the time or inclination to grab a coffee for the journey. Suddenly they were leaving their house, walking to the station, buying a coffee and going home again.'

Nick's first cohort, the existing regulars holding onto one of the few enjoyable parts of their commute, are what we might call 'stay-at-home commuters' – people with nowhere to go retaining the habits they had when they did have somewhere to go. The other cohort, those who'd developed a new lockdown habit for a train station coffee, were also stay-at-home commuters, but they'd picked up their habit during lockdown. Not having to go into the office meant they could give themselves permission to stop for a coffee.

Nick's customers weren't the only ones retaining old commuting habits or, indeed, developing new ones. Many cycling commuters were reluctant to give up the opportunity for some pre-work mindfulness and exercise. Some were even cycling the same route that used to take them to work, but coming back, doing the outbound and homebound leg of their commute in one go. And for every cycle commuter sticking with it during lockdown, it seemed there was someone else getting into the habit, as cycling boomed during lockdown

In the United States, trail riding increased threefold in March 2020 compared to March 2019, cycling increased by 35 per cent in London (Bernhard, 2020) and between April and June 2020 UK bicycle sales increased by 63 per cent year on year (Reid, 2020). So, too, did pet ownership – the Pet Food Manufacturers Association estimated that 2.1 million people got a new pet during lockdown.

The switch to remote work has resulted in some obvious and almost unavoidable lifestyle improvements. The absence of a commute has given people a portion of their day back and many are simply reclaiming that time for leisure. There's more to it, though, than simple allocation of time. There's a shift in mindset, too. People are re-evaluating what's possible when they're not required on-site. And organizations are evaluating what's possible too.

Office space

Without banking and financial sector staff streaming into London's Square Mile every day for work, there simply weren't enough people about to support the various service sector businesses like coffee shops. As of May 2021 there were just 7,850 residential buildings in London's Square Mile, at the heart of the city's financial district (Partridge, 2020). It's one of the most inaccessible and expensive property markets in the world. Between April 2017 and March 2018, just seven new homes were built here. By 2030 there should be 1,500 more homes in the area, thanks simply to the sheer number of vacant offices. The City of London Corporation announced its plan to boost housing stock by 20 per cent, citing its need to respond to 'post-pandemic economic and social trends'. The City of London Corporation had been in consultation with organizations of all sizes 'to understand how the pandemic has affected their ways of working and their needs going forward', according to its policy chair, Catherine McGuinness. 'Firms have told us that they remain committed to retaining a central London hub but how they operate will inevitably change to reflect post-pandemic trends, such as hybrid and flexible working' (Partridge, 2020).

A new frontier in a tedious culture war

One of the more surprising ways working from home has permeated our culture is that it has become something of a fault line in an emerging culture war, a symbol of state control and a reminder of lockdown. Attitudes to the government response to Covid-19 vary massively, but there have been two broad cohorts that can be split based on the intensity of their desire for things to 'get back to normal'. Like masks, some people see working from home as anathema to things getting back to normal. It's a continuation of the restrictions that ruined businesses, put lives on hold and made the world an isolated, dismal place.

Businessman Lord Alan Sugar views home working as a sign of complacency (Waheed, 2021). Conservative pundit and internet publisher Darren Grimes goes a step further and speculates that working from home amounts to us 'losing part of our humanity' (Talk Radio, 2021). He suggests: 'We need to unmuzzle ourselves. We need to get back into our offices because there's so much at stake here. For people my age who are just coming through the workforce it's just so important to have that office atmosphere because you bounce ideas off of colleagues and you pick up new tricks of the trade.'

Grimes was talking to Talk Radio using video conferencing software, from home, where he works. The UK had lifted restrictions by this point, so Grimes could theoretically have been operating from an office. Yet he was more than happy to repeat some of the most popular talking points in favour of getting people back into offices while seemingly enjoying the remote life himself. He raises a fair point: isolation from colleagues can have a negative impact on mental health for some people. That fact, however, shouldn't be used to guilt people back into the office, and we shouldn't overlook the fact that for others, exposure to colleagues can have an equally negative impact on mental health. Working from home will have been a relief for those people. One respondent to Lord Sugar's accusation of complacency summarized the travails of their commute as reason alone to continue with the remote approach: 'Yeah. I want to ride on a packed train for an hour and a half each way so the sandwich shop can charge me £15 for a sandwich, a packet of crisps and small can of Diet Coke. Sounds like an awesome plan' (Waheed, 2021).

Managers need to be mindful of the potential for factional tensions that can lead to petty workplace conflicts if left unresolved. Some people will be desperate to continue working from home after it is safe to return to the office, and other people will judge them for it. Getting away from the office doesn't necessarily mean getting away from office politics. A healthy distributed culture relies on cooperation and buy-in from both office-based and distributed team members.

Fostering a sense of fairness

One of the biggest barriers to cooperation between people who work remotely and people who work in an office is the sense that one group is missing out on something the other group has.

Working remotely must not be allowed to become ideological; most workers will be 'centrist' in their approach to how and where they work, favouring a blend that best suits their lifestyle. A YouGov poll of 4,000 people working from home during the Covid-19 pandemic conducted in July 2021 found that 51 per cent wanted either an equal split or to work from home 'most days'. Only 15 per cent wanted to work from home all of the time. Thomas Kessler, CEO of workplace consultancy Locatee, who commissioned the research, told *The Times*, 'The expectations of office workers have shifted enormously over the last 12 months' (Hosking, 2021).

Organizations that treat remote work as an ideological matter – not including traditionally remote-first businesses that have spent years perfecting their processes and culture and have attracted people on that basis – risk alienating the majority of people who occupy the centre ground where a hybrid approach works best for them.

Inflexible organizations also risk losing talent. The YouGov poll found that 80 per cent of workers wanted some degree of flexibility from employers around working remotely. Yet 24 per cent said their employer was demanding they return to the office full time, and 42 per cent of those polled said being forced back into the office would be a resigning matter (Hosking, 2021). Polling isn't reality, but those figures are worth pondering. For every organization resisting the switch to remote and hybrid working, there's an organization ready to provide a new home to their staff.

05

Work–life integration

When asked what she'd miss most about working from home if she returned to the office full time, the BBC's Amy Williams is quick to point to two simple but important improvements to her life that were only possible because she wasn't office-based. 'I would miss my kitchen and picking up the kids from school without any hassle. Before remote working, I would be stuck in traffic and by the time I picked them up they'd be hungry and in a bad mood. And I'd be in a bad mood too.'

Work obviously has the potential to put us in a bad mood whether we're in an office or working from a sunny beach. But the routines enforced on us by having to work in a certain place between certain hours have the capacity to not only put us in a bad mood, but to adopt unhealthy and negative habits for life. Instead of balancing the competing needs to finish her work and collect her children from school, Williams has integrated them. Which neatly illustrates the core point of this chapter. We talk a lot about work–life balance, but 'balance' implies the even distribution of weight or force, or, worse still, the off-setting of values and benefits. Work–life *integration* is what Amy has been able to achieve since working from home. She doesn't need to rush to the car, or leave work unfinished, in order to collect her kids. Cary has written a whole book on the subject which focuses on work–life integration in the traditional, office-based context. This chapter is for exploring the ideas of integration, only facilitated by working remotely at least part of the time.

Without the requirement to be in a centralized workplace, there are numerous areas of life that can now overlap with work whereas before they couldn't. Collecting children is just one example. We've spoken to lots of people about their experiences of working away from the office. Some of the work–life integrations they've introduced are genuinely impressive: pet ownership, a new fitness regimen, cooking, rediscovering a love of playing guitar, even international travel in one case, as the person in question decided at the first opportunity to relocate to Spain while working remotely. It's not just the extra time people have because they're not commuting that has made these things possible. It's the flexibility that goes with it.

The organizations that stand to benefit the most from the remote working revolution are the ones that understand and take advantage of the work–life opportunities that flexible, remote working brings. Organizations now have an opportunity to give their people what they've been saying they want to give them for years.

Zorica is a search engine optimization (SEO) specialist at a global money transfer platform. Although she's keen to take advantage of the benefits of remote working, Zorica understands that it requires self-discipline. 'Remote work can do wonders for work–life balance but it can also decrease it if you don't put certain systems in place. Working and living in the same space made it very difficult for me to unplug, so I ended up working more than my usual work hours. You really get in the mode of "I'll just do this one extra thing and I'm done", but this is not very healthy in the long run.

'I came up with a few tricks of my own to combat this habit. I set up a dedicated home office area in my flat, and I scheduled activities or arrange to meet people right after I've finished working.'

One thing that helps Zorica go deep in her work and focus on outcomes is that she has a very clear understanding of how her performance is being measured. 'When considering performance we care about just three important metrics,' she explains. These metrics are interlinked. Zorica outlines exactly how her performance is assessed and how they feed into one another. 'Our key metrics are as follows: the amount of traffic our content attracts [in the industry this is described as "monthly organic visits" and refers to the number of people who discover Zorica's articles naturally via a search engine, as opposed to paid channels], the number of users that convert and become customers and the volume of content we can publish in pursuit of the first two goals.'

Zorica manages a team of in-house and freelance writing staff. She also has clearly defined metrics for their outputs. 'We typically publish around 40 pieces of content per person per quarter. And we also create quarterly content plans by conducting keyword research. Since SEO takes time we usually give most projects about six months to kick off before coming up with any serious conclusions about the performance of that content.'

Bringing your whole self to working remotely

It might seem counterintuitive, but one theme that has been mentioned a few times in the interviews we've conducted is how remote working has facilitated greater authenticity. We naturally present a version of ourselves at work that conceals part of who we really are. We unconsciously erase parts of our personas; we cover up our tattoos, wear our hair in a 'professional' style and avoid talking about the more colourful parts of our lives for fear of alienating people. Many of us have simply got used to putting on our work clothes and adopting our work persona to get through the day in as 'professional' a manner as possible. Some of us even have a 'work voice'. Remote working is giving people the power to bring more of themselves (or their non-work selves) to work.

'The need for authenticity has become more pronounced with me,' says Amy. 'When I'm at the office, there's an element of me that feels like I need to act and dress a certain way as a leader and as a woman in a male-dominated environment. But working from home, when you've got a three-year-old bouncing into the room and your husband bringing you a sandwich, it highlights your own reality. I've certainly felt that I've been my authentic self more while at home.'

The need to enforce freedom

When MediaCityUK opened in 2007 in Salford, England, it was seen as a very modern place to work. It didn't have 'offices', it had 'innovation hubs' and 'collaboration zones'. Originally designed as a home for TV studios, media companies and education institutes, it's now home to hundreds of companies, from AI manufacturers to PR firms. One of this book's authors works there, out of a colourfully decorated 'workspace' overlooking the BBC studios. The main purpose of the development was to continue the rejuvenation of the previously derelict Salford Quays area, and to rebalance the London-centric nature of the UK media industry. Some of the UK's largest media brands moved in and set up homes away from home there.

One employee of one of those large media brands relocated to Salford from London when her employer opened a new studio there in 2009. She was excited, expecting her working days to look a lot different to what she was used to. 'When MediaCity opened, it was supposed to be a new way of working; hot desking, mobile phones, laptops, flexible hours and so on. Yet people almost immediately defaulted to working from nine to five, sitting at the same desk. It was disappointing. The environment was different, but the habits remained the same. If you're trying to implement a new way of working, it needs to be empowered, almost enforced. For change to happen as desired, organizations have to establish new habits quickly, otherwise people will cling onto old ways of working because they know doing that is judgement-free.'

The saying 'nobody gets fired for buying IBM' has been around since the 1970s and it's still true today. If you buy your computers from IBM and something goes wrong, it's not your fault. You bought them from IBM. It must be something else that went wrong. The phrase has the same energy as the problem described above. In a nutshell, it's easier to stick with the status quo. If things go wrong, nobody can judge you for doing what millions of other people have been doing for generations. If you try doing things differently and it goes wrong, people will immediately question your judgement.

That's why employers need to be firm when implementing policies that effectively give their people more freedom, otherwise there's a huge risk that most employees will simply avoid taking advantage of said new freedoms and – worse still – will be on the road to burning out. Consider unlimited paid vacation days. Lots of employers used to offer this as a remedy for burnout and most research tells us that it is a flawed policy that fails on two fronts: trust in employers; and boundary-setting by employees.

Ben Gateley, CEO and co-founder of human resources software company CharlieHR, experimented with unlimited paid leave for three years. After the third year, his company reverted back to a traditional policy of setting a maximum number of days for employees based on how long they'd been at the company. Explaining the decision in a company blog, Gateley illustrated the numerous unintended consequences of 'liberating' his employees from a fixed number of paid leave days. In particular, he was concerned that employees weren't taking enough leave because they didn't want to seem uncommitted and had no frame of reference for what was normal. 'Without that numerical allowance, there's no visual cue for you to refer to, no number hanging over your head' (Gateley, 2018).

Some firms attempted to counteract the main problem of people not taking enough time off by setting a minimum number of days their employees had to take, but there were still problems. Josh Pigford, CEO of San Francisco analytics firm Baremetrics, told the BBC in an interview about the practice: 'The reality is, there are boundaries, like, you can't take all year off. So this results in people not taking time off or there being some animosity towards others who some might perceive as taking too much time off' (Yang, 2020).

Preventing burnout is fundamentally about boundary setting. It's all well and good setting a minimum, but the maximum remains unspoken and opaque. An employee who genuinely needs an extended period of leave will always be forced to wrestle with the fear that they're taking advantage of the policy, or letting down their colleagues. A policy that was initially designed to increase employee wellbeing and freedom has ended up restricting it and introducing more problems than it solves. Unlimited holidays generally mean people take less holiday than they'd have been entitled to under a traditional arrangement. Giving them 30 days a year means they'll take 30 days a year because they know the number of days holiday they take will not attract judgement.

Preventing burnout

A report by the think-tank Autonomy published in August 2021 warned that the switch to working from home presented a risk to employees of burnout, due to a blurring of home and work. Will Stronge, Director of Research at Autonomy, said: 'The Covid pandemic has accelerated the need to create much clearer boundaries between work-life and home-life. By enshrining a right to disconnect in British law, workers will be able to take back some control of their lives. British workers put in longer full-time hours than most of Europe and action is needed at the level of government to address these fundamentally unsustainable working conditions' (Jones and Bano, 2021).

The risks are not borne evenly. An earlier report by the same think-tank published in 2020 revealed that women were 43 per cent more likely than men to work more hours while out of the office (Murray, 2020). And they were more likely to have suffered mental health problems because of it.

To prevent an epidemic of burnout, employers of remote teams will have to go further than simply following government policy. They will need to be as firm with freedoms as they are with restrictions, otherwise they risk undermining their workforce's confidence that they will make decisions that are in employees' best interests. When France introduced a law in 2017 protecting workers' right to disconnect, it proved this. Prior to the law coming into force, France was like the rest of the world. Bosses could email their subordinates at any time of day or on the weekend, and even with a friendly 'not urgent' disclaimer they've succeeded in intruding into the private world of their employee. It's almost impossible to not think about the email your boss just sent you. Some bosses do this deliberately, even before they've hired you. In 2017 the boss of online publisher Barstool Sports, Erika Nardini, told *The New York Times* about one of her more intrusive recruitment habits. 'Here's something I do: If you're in the process of interviewing with us, I'll text you about something at 9 p.m. or 11 a.m. on a Sunday just to see how fast you'll respond' (Bryant, 2017).

Most bosses do it by accident. The law in France made it a legal requirement for firms with more than 50 staff to publish a charter so that employees knew when they are expected to respond to emails. But, even then, saying 'We don't expect you to respond to emails after 6 pm' is very, very different to saying 'We expect you *not to* respond to emails after 6 pm.'

German car maker Daimler had a better approach. Instead of asking its workers to set up an out-of-office response when they were away from their desk, they created a piece of software that automatically deleted emails arriving at an inbox when the recipient wasn't supposed to be reading them, sending an automated response to the sender telling them that the message had been deleted and the recipient would never see it, and to try again when the intended recipient was back at their desk. This approach solved three big problems for Daimler. The first and most obvious was that it stopped people reading, responding to and thinking about work emails while away from work. Second, it meant that when they got back to the office they didn't face the stress of hundreds of unread messages. Third, the sender couldn't use the sent email as a means to consider a task done. Upon receiving the automated response, they were given two options: send the email again when the recipient is back, or send it to a colleague if it's urgent.

One of the disadvantages of having a distributed, remote workforce is that the visual and social cues that tell us it's time to stop working are less obvious, or non-existent. It is so much easier to work to a point of exhaustion when you can't see your colleagues physically leaving the office for the day, or heading out to get lunch.

Without rigidly enforced boundaries, wellness policies get ignored. Employers are pretty good at enforcing policies that are restrictive, but not so good at enforcing policies that are liberating, even if they have the best intentions. Take internet usage policies. Most employers discourage their people from logging into social media or eBay during office hours, but not all of them prevent it. Many employers accept that their staff may occasionally use the internet for personal reasons while at work and, after weighing up the cost of writing and enforcing a policy to stop them versus the risks of letting it slide, will decide that a bit of extra-curricular browsing is preferable to having to discipline someone for checking Facebook for five minutes. Any employer that really doesn't want its staff browsing social media websites during office hours can easily justify a filter that prevents them doing just that.

The same should be true in reverse. Employers that genuinely want their staff to avoid burnout need to think carefully about which policies they want to encourage and which policies they want to enforce. Tools already exist to prevent us from getting distracted. Browser plugins like Momentum, StayFocused and Be Timeful are all great for making it either hard or impossible to dip into distracting websites. They simply block browser access for a specific amount of time and make it hard for users to get around their restrictions.

Employers seeking to make sure their people aren't over-functioning could very easily repurpose this kind of technology to prevent overwork. Flexibility is great, and some workers prefer to operate in bursts of activity that may see them breach what their employer considers a healthy amount of time at their desk. And that's not the sort of behaviour we're trying to discourage. Employers should be able to tell the difference between a worker who can only get stimulated when there's a deadline looming and a worker who is persistently putting in more hours than they should. Technological interventions that make it hard for everyone, especially anxious or over-functioning employees, to persistently overwork will be as useful an addition to the remote working toolkit as video conferencing and instant messages.

Ross, who we heard from in previous chapters, credits his company's firm stance on preventing burnout as a big contributor to the levels of trust he has in them to adapt to the distributed model.

'They've cracked down hard on people working excess hours, as the temptation is to work ever more overtime to catch up on your work. Generally, I think the senior leadership team have done a good job on this one. Personally, I haven't felt pressured to work more hours than I'm contracted to.

'We have daily meetings and we also have tea breaks three times a week where we don't talk about work. Personally, I've arranged catch-ups with most of my team where we chat off the record about work. In my chats none of them have expressed any concerns about working from home, aside from the usual comments about missing the office environment.

'Most of us are parents and live with family, so we do have lives outside of our work. I do feel that those in the team that live on their own have struggled throughout the lockdowns, but that's likely lifted alongside the restrictions.

'I think the company and the senior leadership team have done about as well as could be expected under the circumstances. They've really tried to foster a culture where everyone feels they can speak and, ironically, since working from home I've probably spoken more to my senior management than before. I think that some colleagues are always going to favour the physical interactions and I've missed them as well. Certainly within my team we always get contributions from every colleague, not just the senior and experienced people like myself. It's a bit different, though, when we have department-wide meetings, which have around 100 people involved.

'They put a real focus on our mental health over the last year and the leadership team have encouraged more flexible working practices. It sounds grand, but what this means in practice is that they're encouraging us to take longer lunches so we can exercise and spend time in our gardens.'

The discourse around work–life balance and work–life integration can be quite toxic. When it comes to discussing hours worked and boundary setting, the debate inevitably becomes a proxy battle between employers and employees. And it's not always the employers you might suspect who go hardest into this debate. Every so often someone delivers a point of view with such bluntness that the content of their entire argument becomes obscured by the manner in which they claim to have arrived at one particular opinion. In an August 2021 article for *Fortune* magazine, a relatively unknown contributor, in arguing the case against workers setting boundaries, effectively admitted firing someone for not working outside of his contracted hours. 'I recently fired my first-ever direct report,' the author explains. 'Although he was low-energy, uninspired, and an awful speller, what ultimately led him to the ax was his insistence on boundaries. He would come into the office at nine every morning, leave at five, and be inaccessible anytime before and after' (Peterson, 2021).

The article, entitled 'Want to work 9-to-5? Good luck building a career', understandably upset a lot of people. The author's attitude to the employee she fired came across as dismissive and disrespectful. But she also made some reasonable arguments that may not have reached such a large audience had her opening confession not been so controversial. The article's main assertion – that refusing to be flexible and work outside of your agreed hours may be your right, but it will harm your career – hinges on what the author calls the 'pursuit of equity' between work and life becoming distorted into a sense of entitlement. Peterson argues in her piece that there's a trade-off to be had, and that since work is part of life, expecting the work–life balance to entail total separation between the two is unrealistic. She makes a point worth contemplating.

Peterson cited an example of an employee leaving the office to deal with a personal matter. Excluding matters of grave personal importance such as a sick relative, for which there is no workplace equivalent, Peterson argues that there should be give and take in both directions; if your boss lets you come in late because you've got a tradesperson visiting in the morning, then surely you should be prepared to reciprocate the next time your boss needs your attention outside of office hours. After all, isn't this what flexibility is all about?

Sort of, but not quite. There's a very obvious power dynamic between bosses and their subordinates. While the boss may seem benevolent by cheerfully agreeing to a request for a tradesperson-related late start, it is likely that the boss would not need to ask at all, in the same circumstances. Employees understand this, and probably hate having to ask at all, knowing their boss has more autonomy than them. A boss can build rapport and earn trust from their more junior direct reports by handling these sorts of requests in a friendly and empathetic manner. And indeed it may help the boss feel good about themselves too. But to the employee, no matter how cheerfully approved their informal absence request might be, there's always the concern that it *could* be denied and there'd be very little they could do about it. They also know that their boss is probably, maybe unintentionally, keeping a mental ledger of how many informal requests for absence each employee makes. It's why some employees buy into the theory that it's easier to apologise than to ask permission. If managers knew how many car breakdowns, late trains or other 'unavoidable' sources of delay were actually planned absences for which their employee didn't want to seek formal approval, they might be surprised.

Peterson blames 'hustle culture', a toxic habit normalized by the sort of celebrity CEOs who post their morning routines on LinkedIn, for an increase in burnout. And she rightly points out that many organizations took full advantage of the combination of financial precariousness brought about by the 2008 financial crash and the urge to be seen to be hungry and ambitious to encourage anxious workers to over-function. At its conclusion Peterson's argument becomes less persuasive. She appears to be challenging an argument that nobody is actually making – that workers don't appreciate the value of 'toxic productivity' to their long-term career goals.

Creating a remote environment

So where will most people actually be working in the hybrid future, and how can employers support their people to create the best environments?

From the office

One of the most compelling arguments for retaining the status quo of full-time office attendance as standard is that, without it, organizations and their people would suffer from a lack of opportunities to collaborate. While compelling on the surface, this argument is less than convincing when you dig deeper. For a start, it's probably not productive or fair to compare the scope for collaboration between off-site and on-site contexts until we've had the time to develop and refine the very promising remote collaboration tools and techniques that have emerged during the various global lockdowns. Let's not forget that a lot of what got businesses through those periods was improvised, cobbled together and deployed in the context of one of the biggest economic disruptions in living memory. We need time before we can fairly judge the merits and flaws of remote collaboration.

Perhaps more importantly, there's a good chance that we're overstating the traditional office's capacity for supporting meaningful collaboration. Especially now we have to contemplate giving up the form of office collaboration we've grown used to. One of the biggest detriments to workplace collaboration in recent times was the popularity of the open plan office. The 'widespread refusal to return to pre-pandemic office standards can be largely attributed to the failures of the open-office concept' notes product designer and interior architect Alejandra Albarran in a 2021 piece for *Fast Company* entitled 'Open offices failed. These are 6 essentials to make sure the next office doesn't'. Albarran's contempt for the open-plan office is rooted in its failure to deliver what it promised. Open-plan offices, she argues, were 'designed to foster more collaboration and socialization across company departments, but gave little consideration to the variety of working environments necessary for a comfortable, productive workplace'.

Multiple studies back her up. One study published in the *Harvard Business Review* found that when firms switched to open-plan offices, face-to-face interactions fell by 70 per cent. 'Many common assumptions about office architecture and collaboration are outdated or wrong. Although the open-office design is intended to encourage us to interact face-to-face, it gives us permission not to' (Bernstein and Waber, 2019). That's the scathing conclusion of Associate Professor in the Organizational Behavior Unit at the Harvard Business School, Ethan Bernstein, and Visiting Scientist at the Massachusetts Institute of Technology Media Lab, Ben Waber. The 'accidental collisions' facilitated by open-plan offices and free spaces can be counter-productive. In many instances, 'co-presence' via an open-plan office or a digital channel does not result in productive collaboration. Keep in mind Bernstein and Waber's take-down of open-plan offices wasn't written as a post-justification for sticking with remote work now that we've had a taste of it – their study was written in 2019. It's a detailed examination of the flaws and assumptions we've been making about this style of working for years, and not an argument in favour of remote working per se. In fact, they have some fairly strong observations on the limitations of remote working, too, especially for projects that demand regular interaction between colleagues. 'While studying a major technology company from 2008 to 2012, we found that remote workers communicated nearly 80 per cent less about their assignments than colocated team members did; in 17 per cent of projects they didn't communicate at all' (Bernstein and Waber, 2019). While a robust observation, it doesn't necessarily suggest remote working and office are equally limiting contexts for collaboration. And when we consider that most organizations will adopt a blend of on-site and off-site working, we don't need to treat this as a tug-of-war between two competing work styles. But this point does underscore the neutrality and subjectivity of Bernstein and Waber's research.

Perhaps the most interesting area of their research lies in the story behind open-plan offices, rather than their relative utility as incuba-tors of effectiveness. According to Bernstein and Waber, the open-plan revolution was simply a matter of cost and the dynamic relationship between headcounts and floor space. 'During much of the 1990s, organizations hired employees faster than they expanded their offices. With layoffs in the early 2000s recession, and again in 2008, surviv-ing workers regained some space, largely because companies held long-term leases and were loath to invest in office reconfigurations.

But as hiring rebounded, leases came due, and redesign budgets recovered, organizations again began fitting their people into smaller and smaller spaces.'

Offices have been changing for years. Cubicles used to be the standard configuration. Then open plan. Then hot desking. Whatever the format, we still need offices and the office still has a major role to play in the hybrid working future. It may no longer form the nexus of the working world and its function will undoubtedly change, but the office isn't going away any time soon. The first challenge organizations will face is deciding what role they want their offices to play in their future and what they're going to do with the space they no longer need. By August 2021 major organizations were already sharing their plans. A survey by *The Times* of the 100 most valuable businesses listed on the London Stock Exchange found that the overwhelming majority of firms planned to adopt hybrid working (Greenwood et al, 2021). Just one firm out of a hundred surveyed, the steel and mining company Evraz, said it planned to return all of its previously office-based staff to its London headquarters full time, albeit with a phased reintroduction. Sage Group PLC, the firm behind a range of popular business software products, revealed that it was going to treat its office spaces as collaboration hubs, renaming them 'Sage hubs', and would be relaxing its requirement for staff to attend the office all the time. It also announced that staff would be able to work for ten weeks of the year from wherever they liked (Greenwood et al, 2021).

The Times survey proved that firms were prepared to tolerate empty space in their offices. Before the Covid-19 pandemic, this would have made little financial sense for businesses paying expensive office rents and rates. The prevailing model has always been to optimize floor space to manage real estate costs. But the world is different now. The distance between your desk and the desk nearest to you will have an extremely powerful influence on how comfortable you feel about returning to work. It will affect your perceptions of how your employer values your health and comfort. And companies, to their credit, have figured this out pretty quickly. BP told *The Times* it would operate a 60/40 home/office model to free up space in its offices. Abrdn (formerly Standard Life Aberdeen plc) said it would operate its offices at no more than 30 per cent capacity. Of course, this is only an option to larger firms with the financial means to absorb what is effectively 'wasted' floor space. Smaller firms, and firms for whom their corporate real estate represents a more significant overhead, will have to be more creative or radical. Many may decide that safely and comfortably operating offices in expensive buildings in expensive cities no longer makes business sense. And for firms committed to a hybrid model that doesn't demand 100 per cent occupancy 100 per cent of the time, that may open up new opportunities. Hubs in less expensive rural areas, short-term contracts and rotating headquarters or creative use of networked co-working spaces may all be solutions to the problem.

Another option for firms with offices they don't want to give up is flexible scheduling. We've explored the opportunities afforded by remote working as they relate to the places we work and the times we work. It is possible to mix and match the two. Assuming an organization has no intention of distributing its workforce geographically, it can still embrace part of the distributed working ethos and avoid having offices at full capacity. Not everyone does their best work between the hours of nine and five, and there are plenty of workers who will appreciate the chance to be more flexible not only with the days they work but also the hours. Parents of young children are an obvious use case. Instead of demanding that parents fit childcare duties around work, allowing them to work non-traditional hours in the office lets them fit work around childcare. For parents of preschool and school-age children, this could completely eliminate the immense stress of combining the school run with the commute.

The next challenge organizations will face as they roll out their own version of the hybrid model is re-acquainting their people with office working, and more specifically the version of office working they want to take forward. Adequate spacing between desks is a big, important gesture that will signal a company's commitment to their people's comfort and health, but it's not an option for all firms and it isn't enough on its own.

It will be a case of trial and error. During the height of the pandemic, in workplaces that had to stay open, including banks, shops and offices for essential services, the Perspex screen became a ubiquitous symbol of 'good' health and safety practice – a physical barrier protecting workers from harmful airborne microbes and also a strong visual indicator that the people in charge were doing their best. Or at least, doing something. The efficacy of these screens isn't necessarily as obvious as we might assume. There were still outbreaks of Covid-19 in workplaces that used them, and the science around whether they adequately protect people isn't settled (Meyersohn, 2020). And there's also the fact that the presence of screens reduces compliance with other more effective measures of reducing the spread of viruses, such as mask wearing. 'We know so much more now, and we follow the scientific data to guide our decisions,' said a spokesperson for the FMI, a trade group for the United States grocery industry, in October 2020 (Meyersohn, 2020). 'Based on the recommendations by public health authorities, it would be important to look at layered controls in any environment.'

Simple but non-obvious things matter too. For example, one thing that we noticed about public buildings that were open during the pandemic was that their signage and way-marking was inadequate to the point of being actively harmful to people's health. Consider a building with a new, ad hoc layout and one-way system designed to keep people from congregating or being unnecessarily face-to-face. Now consider that nobody in the building is 100 per cent sure of which way to go, which doors are now exits, which areas are restricted and the only way to find out is to read a sign. But the writing on the sign is too small to read from a distance of more than 6 feet. So the only way to get the information you need about safely moving around the building is to stand close enough to the sign to read it without breathing on the five other people who are also desperate to know how to remain safe while moving around the building. You can see the problem. Signage and way-marking in offices will need radically rethinking in order to help people feel comfortable.

One solution that caused a lot of debate was the use of colour-coded lanyards for employers to communicate what levels of physical contact, if any, they were comfortable with. It's not clear who actually pioneered the idea but plenty of firms, including retirement and savings provider Phoenix Group and education company Oxbridge Home Learning, both announced that they're trying it out.

As more people get vaccinated and the virus that has done so much to accelerate the remote working revolution abates, people will naturally become less concerned by what their employers are doing to keep them from catching it. But they will still want to feel safe and they will want to be reassured that their employers take their health and comfort seriously. What employees will not want, however, is intrusive and ultimately pointless 'hygiene theatre'. Essayist and contributor to *The Atlantic*, Derek Thompson, coined the phrase in 2020, during the peak of the pandemic. 'National restaurants such as Applebee's are deputizing sanitation czars to oversee the constant scrubbing of window ledges, menus, and high chairs. The gym chain Planet Fitness is boasting in ads that "there's no surface we won't sanitize, no machine we won't scrub." New York City is shutting down its subway system every night, for the first time in its 116-year history, to blast the seats, walls and poles with a variety of antiseptic weaponry, including electrostatic disinfectant sprays. And in Wauchula, Florida, the local government gave one resident permission to spray the town with hydrogen peroxide as he saw fit. "I think every city in the damn United States needs to be doing it," he said' (Thompson, 2020).

It's understandable during a pandemic that everyone wanted to be seen to be doing something, but that urge to satisfy optics can quickly morph into something pointless and less than useful. You've probably seen examples of it yourself and you may have even participated in someone else's hygiene theatre production; one-way systems that do nothing to limit close contact and enforced hand-sanitizing in badly ventilated spaces being two common examples. Organizations must resist the urge to do this.

From home

Setting aside for a moment the really obvious benefits of working from home, one benefit that merits much consideration is the potential for personalization. And, for what it's worth, personalization is important to workers. To explore this area effectively, it's useful to describe the two types of personalization people value. There's the traditional, superficial type of personalization – family photos on desks and perhaps a pot plant and a favourite coffee cup. And then there's the deeper, but no more significant type (pictures and coffee mugs are very important to the people that make the effort to personalize their workspaces) that involves things like lighting, seating, audio, temperature and colours. Traditional personalization used to be relatively common, and the degree to which you might personalize your workspace was related to your status; someone with their own office might have been able to hang a favourite painting on the wall, someone with their own cubicle might have had to make do with a 4x5 inch framed photo of their family. As workplaces modernized, scope for personalization dwindled and a gulf in the scope of personalization emerged between the managerial class and their subordinates. The decline of the much-maligned office cubicle, ostensibly done for the good of the workforce but more likely a cost-cutting measure, took away a lot of opportunities for personalization. Without the three walls of a cubicle, no matter how symbolically restrictive they may have been, there was nowhere to pin photographs and other personal bits and pieces. The shift to open-plan working still allowed for some degree of personalization; people could still have photos on their desks but did so knowing the rest of the office could see them. But with hot desking, the idea that you could turn a workspace into something you felt ownership of was ultimately killed off.

This might seem trivial but it's not. 'Most contemporary offices are functional and offer very little user control, but our studies suggest this practice needs to be challenged' (University of Exeter, 2010) says Dr Craig Knight, who conducted a study into workplace personalization at the University of Exeter. The study found that those 'working in enriched spaces were 17 per cent more productive than those in lean spaces, but those sitting at empowered desks were even more efficient – being 32 per cent more productive than their lean counterparts without any increase in errors'. It plays into the concept of bringing your whole self to work. It may be, as the BBC's Amy Williams said in Chapter 4, that now people are working from home more often, they're able to bring more of themselves to work.

The deeper type of personalization that could never have happened in an office has great potential to make working a significantly more rewarding, comfortable and productive endeavour. And there are significant implications here for accessibility and equality, too. One example is the ambient temperature of offices. Have you ever been in an office on a hot day and noticed your women colleagues bundled up in jumpers and scarves? If you have, you might have wondered why. The reason, as it was explained back in 2015, is that thermostats are 'sexist'. That is to say, thermostats are based on the needs of a '40-year-old man weighing about 154 pounds' using a 'thermal comfort model that was developed in the 1960s' (Belluck, 2015). Of course, the model on which modern thermostats operate hasn't changed in the six or so decades since it was developed. But workplaces have. They're now full of women, as well as men.

The sexual politics of the office is too big a subject to get into in this book, and frankly it is far outside of our scope. But what we can confidently say is that if the opportunities for personalization lead to liberation from the many inbuilt inequalities of office life – including sex, age, disability specifically – then, if it achieves nothing else in terms of productivity, the switch to remote working will have been worthwhile. Obviously, personalization of space does not represent the limit of the capabilities of remote working, but it's a great start.

At 'the third workplace'

The idea of 'the third place' was popularized by Ray Oldenburg in his book *The Great Good Place: Cafes, coffee shops, bookstores, bars, hair salons, and other hangouts at the heart of a community* (1989). Oldenburg argues the importance of social settings that are separate from the two so-called most important places in an adult's life – their home and their place of work. Oldenburg cites pubs, coffee houses, parks, churches and even main streets as quintessential third places that naturally foster socialization and community. These can be great places for working.

Alejandra Albarran, the workspace designer who was so scathing about open-plan offices earlier in this chapter, has a theory about third places straddling the line between social and work. She calls them 'third workplaces' (Albarran, 2021). 'The third workplace is helping to bridge a gap that many employees are feeling when it comes to settling on an ideal working environment.'

She notes in her 2021 article for *Fast Company* that organizations are already onto the idea of supporting their workers find productivity in unofficial workplaces outside of the home, observing that 'companies are turning to the concept of a third workplace, which fits well into the hybrid work model – allowing employees to choose a dynamic space that provides perks, amenities, and designated areas for focus work and socialization not often found at home or in the traditional office. Third workplaces fill the gap at an individual level as the place you choose to do your best work' (Albarran, 2021).

For anyone that's already tried the third place approach, there are a number of obvious benefits. Nathan opted for different coffee places. These are great because, aside from the cost of the drinks, they're free. If you live anywhere even remotely metropolitan, there's abundant choice, and they are specifically designed to be nice, comfortable spots for relaxing. Coffee shops let you mix up your routine and your surroundings and they're sufficiently informal that you can blur the lines between being at work and being 'out', which, despite what many opposed to working from anywhere other than an office might say, isn't necessarily a bad thing.

There are drawbacks too, of course, and they're the sort you don't necessarily anticipate until you've tried working from one yourself. The first drawback is the lack of control you have over your environment. Some things you can predict, some you can't. There will be music playing and a general hum of social activity, but these are usually at a volume that provides nothing more than a white noise effect. But not always. Sometimes there will be noisy families and, depending on your luck, people who want to talk to you. Security is a problem, too, both the physical kind and the information kind. Let's look at physical security first. Sean remembers working from a coffee shop in Manchester with a friend who was doing it for the first time. The coffee shop in question (Takk, in Manchester's Northern Quarter) actively catered to people who wanted to work. Aside from fantastic coffee, the venue provided a plug at each table, fast, reliable WiFi that customers could use without giving up any personal data and music designed to aid concentration. Even today, if you were to pop into this particular coffee shop, you'd probably count no fewer than 10 high-end laptops in use. The friend commented, 'If I was a robber I'd come here before I thought about holding up a Post Office. There must be at least £20,000 worth of technology on these tables, and not a security guard or camera in sight.' It was a valid point, too. For all of the faults we can ascribe to the traditional office, the risk of property crime probably isn't one of them. The point becomes even more relevant when you're working on your own and need the bathroom. Do you take your laptop with you and risk losing a coveted table, do you leave it unaccompanied, or do you ask a trustworthy looking fellow co-worker to keep any eye on it and hope they'll still be there when you return?

Co-working spaces solve part of this problem. The good ones have secure WiFi, door security systems and lockable storage. There's still the issue of confidentiality, as most are open-plan. Commercially sensitive phone calls and private internal calls don't work in an open-plan context when you have no control over who sits within earshot. Some co-working spaces have solved this with private booths for phone calls. But there is a general sense among some of the larger businesses we've spoken to that the style of co-working made popular by firms like WeWork – where informality, collaboration and mixing between businesses is strongly encouraged and effectively part of the design – aren't quite the answer they need. Having spoken to a number of corporations who are actively looking into providing a 'third place' solution, the consensus appears to be that co-working spaces are too 'informal' in the areas that matter to them: information security, privacy and confidentiality. They're not necessarily looking to replicate their existing office environments on a smaller scale, but they do need to keep some of the basics.

There's a big opportunity here for co-working spaces, or at least the people who own the properties that host them. Until very recently, co-working catered almost exclusively to freelancers, small startups and early-stage businesses, often in tech or media. And they've tailored their spaces and peripheral services to cater for these use cases. The ones I've had experience of do a great job of providing add-ons that benefit early-stage businesses: providing introductions to banks and funding providers, workshops and mini-conferences as well as the sort of lifestyle benefits that appeal: discounted gym membership, networking, mindfulness sessions, yoga, wine tasting, free alcohol (unbelievably, this one of the least popular initiatives I've personally witnesses) and life coaching to name a few. These are great for a certain demographic but will probably add very little value to the sort of people who will be seeking out co-working spaces in the very near future – larger corporations looking for 'overspill' space for remote workers for whom working from home isn't a viable option.

Without advocating for corporate outposts catering solely for office overspill, there's a strong business case for providing flexible, basic services that approximate the hard-to-replace, nuts-and-bolts elements of an office. In fact, there is an enormous opportunity to cater directly to the 'I need a desk, secure WiFi and peace and quiet' market that soon may massively outnumber the 'I want to meet other founders in a place that has free beer' market.

Nathan Chew is Head of Venue and Events at the Manchester Chamber of Commerce. Manchester Chamber's business lounge comes as close as I've seen to meeting the demands described above, namely a work space without the add-ons; a location that corporations can use with confidence and with the boring but important stuff like secure internet and spaces for privacy.

'80 per cent of our own staff now work outside of the office,' he explains. 'So we've repurposed the space they're not using and extended our business lounge. We're offering organized, flexible space for people who may be used to working in more traditional offices. It's relaxed and relatively informal, but it's definitely a place of work. There won't be any WeWork style beer taps. We understand that organizations in regulated sectors have certain non-negotiables when it comes to their physical environment and we're aiming to meet some of those needs.'

For the Chamber of Commerce, offering more space now that they have it is a no-brainer. 'We recognized quite early on that doing this would support our reason for existence, which is to build our membership. Our staff will work in and amongst people using our spaces and will be there to offer business and technical support.'

As well as seeing a shift in the working habits of people within his own organization, Chew has been in a position to observe trends among the Chamber's membership and the local business community more generally. And he has a theory about what might happen to some of the other empty corporate real estate that risks going under-utilized now people want to work elsewhere.

'There are a couple of people I know of who are exploring a brokerage model for office space. And it makes total sense to me. You've got organizations with big offices, long leases and a work-force that's quite happy outside of the office. They're wondering what to do with the unused space. Meanwhile you've also got organiza-tions with fewer, if any, real estate obligations with people working remotely who are looking for something that isn't quite an office and isn't quite co-working. This brokerage solution seems logical. Office owners can generate revenue from those empty spaces and businesses can access modular, flexible workspaces.'

Albarrran (2021) believes there's a formula for the ideal third workplace. 'Through both my years spent designing many client workspaces across the world, and the experiences of the many archi-tects, engineers, and product designers that I work alongside, we have found a specific way of space planning to create a truly dynamic workplace. It contains six main categories of space types, which are purposefully created for different types of activities: community, collaboration, meet, team, solo work, and well-being.'

Albarran's vision has parallels with architect David Dewane's controversial concept that he calls the 'Eudaimonia Machine' (Newport, 2016). It's a hypothetical concept of the ideal environment for getting good work done and is based on Aristotle's concept of eudaimonia, which means the epitome of human capability. According to Dewane's idealized Eudaimonia Machine vision, the perfect working environment contains five distinct spaces; gallery, salon, library, office and chamber. Each is designed to facilitate a certain type of behaviour conducive to getting good work done. It's a linear design that forces anyone entering it to go through each space before entering the next. No spaces, and therefore experiences, are optional. The gallery is the first place you enter, and this is for inspiration. Galleries should contain examples of work produced by others using the space, to provide inspiration to the next people that come through. The salon, according to Dewane's concept, would be something akin to a breakout space or reception area. There would be good coffee, comfortable seating and interesting things to look at. This is where casual interactions and networking would happen. Moving through the salon to the library is where things get a bit more serious. The library is for research and, according to Dewane, it would serve as a repository for all of the resources used in the creation in the work that's happened inside the machine. After the library is the office. The office is staffed by an administrator who can help people with resources and guidance. Finally, the worker ends up in a chamber. These are soundproofed and designed for single-occupancy, the perfect environment for working in a state of deep, undistracted focus on a singular task.

Perhaps the most enticing benefit of remote working is the possibility of working anywhere in the world. And this is one instance where culture can be transported. If you're working from home without a hitch, in theory, there's no reason you can't move your home to somewhere nicer or more suited to your lifestyle. It's already happening and governments are cottoning on to the possible benefits to their own economies of welcoming remote workers from around the world. Both Malta and Lanzarote launched campaigns in 2021 to advertise the benefits of relocating as a remote worker.

Measuring success

As tempting as it might be, employers should resist the urge to measure the success of switching to a remote-first model on the sole basis of productivity or quality of work. That's just a small part of a bigger picture. The true benefits of switching to remote working may not reveal themselves for years. And a lot of the benefits are pretty much unplottable. While you can certainly gauge how many sales an employee has made compared to last year, you absolutely can't know whether they were thinking of leaving for a rival company this time last year, but decided to stay because your company went remote and the rival didn't. These intangibles form only a small part of a bigger picture.

There's also the matter of happiness. It may sound simplistic, but happiness is important in and of itself. Big organizations are always banging the drum about wanting happy employees because happy employees make productive workers. That's fine. But let's not forget that we're talking about people here. If embracing and facilitating a genuinely supportive remote culture gives them the opportunity to finally move to the seaside, or get a dog, or spend more time with elderly relatives while they still can, isn't that better still?

06

Wellbeing, environment, inclusion and belonging

We've discussed it already but it's worth repeating: environment and culture are not the same, no matter how often organizations conflate the two. Culture is important and is primarily what this book is concerned with. Environment is important, too, and deserves its own consideration when planning for a distributed workforce. In this chapter we'll explore ways organizations can foster mental wellbeing, leverage remoteness to remove barriers to better physical wellbeing and support employees who want to optimize their physical environments for both wellbeing and work effectiveness.

The case for annualized hours

In their book *Remote: Office not required* (2013), David Heinemeier Hansson and Jason Fried describe the traditional office as an 'interruption factory'. There probably isn't a snappier summing up of the way offices often defeat their own purpose. This isn't to denigrate the office but to shine a light on the opportunities presented by not making it the nexus of where all work gets done. The authors pose the question 'Where do you go when you really need to get work done?'

Due to the pandemic, organizations around the world have rapidly abandoned the idea that their people need to work in a specific place.

Capitalism didn't collapse. If workers don't need to work in a specific place, what's to say they don't need to at a specific time either? If we treated working hours the way Covid-19 forced us to treat office centricity, we could open up another world of new possibilities for how work gets done.

We're not simply advocating for even flexier flexi-time here. There's a case for being as radical in our approach to *when* we work as we've been in our approach to *where* we work.

Annualized hours contracts guarantee a certain number of hours to be worked across a year. These contracts were originally designed to provide a degree of employment security for people in professions with natural fluctuations in demand, like aviation or seasonal work. As flexible working has become more popular, some employers have offered annualized hours contracts to working parents so they can work more during term time and less during school holidays. Some employers offer 'summer hours' where employees work shorter days when the weather is good and make it up over the winter. Most annualized hours contracts are not entirely flexible, however. Employees still need to be 'on site' during a specified range of times, but they can be flexible within those ranges.

Under a traditional contract, a worker understands that their presence, physical or virtual, is expected between two relatively arbitrary start and stop times. Someone who naturally does their best work at night may be less inclined to do it unless they're able to recoup those working hours the following day. If they're contracted to show up somewhere – an office or on Slack – at a certain time, why would they be motivated to work through the night as well? Likewise, someone who performs best in a 'project mindset', doing extended bursts of a few long days or even weeks followed by a period of doing nothing (we're not condoning 'crunch' culture which pervades certain deadline-heavy industries like game design or film editing). If this type of worker is still expected to log in between 8 am and 10 am, Monday to Friday, they're effectively doing free overtime. Yes, most employers offer time in lieu, but that's generally a function of overtime facilitated by having minimum weekly or monthly hours and predicated on a rota system. It would take a brave employee to tell their manager not to expect them because they worked until 2 am on a project deliberately left until the 11th hour because that's how they perform best.

Assuming an annualized contract is based on the typical 37.5 hour working week, accounting for statutory holiday entitlements, a worker owes his or her employer approximately 1,740 hours of their labour in a year, out of a possible 8,760. This means there's more than enough space for workers of different styles to split their work time out in a way that truly suits them.

Annualizing worker hours potentially opens up significant pockets of time outside of evenings and weekends for workers to do other things: go on an intensive language course, learn to cook, train for a marathon. Evenings and weekends are great, but they don't provide enough runway to take on significant commitments outside of work.

Workers could create their own paid sabbaticals or, if they're creative enough, build a mini retirement into their careers. Combined with the time they've already saved by not commuting to a centralized office and the fact that they can theoretically live anywhere they like, the scope for life-changing reconfigurations of work and life is huge. This is a big win for employers too. Numerous studies link contentedness in an employee's personal life with higher levels of motivation and engagement at work.

The power of jacking it in

One of the most damaging habits that's been allowed to develop in the context of the traditional office is what we might call 'performative productivity' – the act of appearing busy to conceal a period of low output. We've all been there. Call it whatever you like: writer's block, absence of flow state, or sometimes – if we're being radically honest – lack of interest in the job at hand. It happens to even the most productive and effective workers.

For whatever reason – and there are many legitimate reasons, such as tiredness, illness, depression, having bigger things to worry about –

the mental state we need to enter to achieve the desired level of productivity evades us and we're faced with having to try to look busy while we wait for inspiration to arrive. This is not healthy or useful.

Productivity isn't linear. It doesn't start at 9 am and end at 5 pm, with two phases of steadily humming output punctuated only by a break for lunch. Productivity comes in spikes at inconvenient times. How often have you struggled with a piece of work for hours only to nail it in 30 minutes the following day?

The office is an unforgiving environment when we can't access the necessary headspace to do what we need to do. So we fake it. We're clocked in and at our desk, ostensibly 'at work', but nothing's happening. Employers know that this happens. It's why the sensible ones have breakout spaces and collaboration areas (and some have ball pits and hammocks). These features are designed to acknowledge that sometimes employees need a change of scene or a screen break, but they keep them firmly inside the office. What employees really need is permission to 'jack it in'. If they're going to be experiencing a period of low productivity, what's the difference if they do it in an expensively designed breakout space or if they do it at an art gallery, park or – dare we say it – the pub?

Remote working partially solves this problem. Outside of the physical constraints of the office, employees are more likely to simply switch off and do something else without the guilt and anxiety they would experience in the office. They might well return to their work feeling refreshed and ready, fully equipped to tackle whatever problem had been confounding them. What workers should do in this scenario is simply 'jack it in'. When you've been staring at the same blank document, presentation or graphic for hours with no return on investment, your time and your employer's money is better spent walking the dog. Instead of resisting this impulse to do something else, employers should be prepared to embrace it.

The freedom to take this approach, though, is necessarily limited by the non-physical confines of office working hours. Our pivot to remote working has, ironically, made this problem worse. As long as we're signed up for something vaguely nine to five-ish across the board, the collaboration tools like Slack and Teams that have been invaluable for distributed teams will have a tethering effect too. Even though you've gone for a walk to clear your head, there's a direct line back to the office in your pocket. Ignore messages for too long and your colleagues will wonder where you are. Or, at the very least, your brain will tell you they're wondering where you are.

Stepping away from the twin constraints of location and office hours frees workers up to optimize their day for maximum productivity. It's not big news that some people get more done early in the morning, others late at night and some people can only really perform when there's a deadline looming immediately over them. Provided the outputs are good, managers shouldn't begrudge these idiosyncrasies. They should embrace them. If an employee can produce good work in the expected volumes using just 80 per cent of their contracted hours, there are two options: give them the space they need during the other 20 per cent of the time, or try to squeeze the remaining drops of value out of them by enforcing their presence for an arbitrary portion of the day.

We acknowledge that if implemented informally, this approach is ripe for abuse. Some workers will simply see it as a framework for slacking off. But if they're prone to slacking off, they'd have already found a way to do that in the office during their contracted nine-to-five shift. The benefits for the ones that don't use it to slack off will surely outweigh the harm done by the slackers. An organizational framework that accounts for productivity-related periods of absence would be harder to abuse because 'jacking in' hours are already baked into the employer's expectations.

Jacking in and slacking off are not the same thing. Jacking in is liberation from performative productivity. It comes from the acceptance that the creative or analytical juices are not always flowing and it provides a healthy framework for capturing productivity when it peaks. Slacking off is a chronic malaise unrelated to an employee's natural productivity rhythm. More likely, an employee who persistently under-delivers is disengaged from their work, inadequately supported by their management, lazy or all three. And they'd be that way working remotely or in the office. Slackers are very good at concealing their tracks.

The importance of digital literacy for belonging

There are journalists working today who can still remember a time when newspaper front pages were literally glued together. And there are publicists working today who can remember a time when press releases were typed up, copied and delivered by courier to every news desk on Fleet Street in the hope of getting a story inside one of those papers. To many younger workers in the media or public relations today, this idea must seem entirely alien. But it's how things were and they were like that for far longer than they've been like this.

The information revolution changed how work got done. Journalists can publish a story to the world from their kitchen table. And publicists can distribute a press release to thousands of journalists at the same time, at the click of a button. That press release can contain high-resolution images, videos and hyperlinks to Dropbox files with yet more assets.

Those journalists and publicists working today who can remember how things were are only working today because they were able to develop a digital skillset. Those that didn't got left behind or retired while younger workers for whom photo editing and video production were something they learned for fun as children overtook them. To get on in the media, public relations, or pretty much any industry, it was imperative to keep up with digital innovations like email, social media and cloud computing.

The remote work skillset will have the same effect as the information technology revolution. For some, sharing a clickable web page prototype on Slack will be as natural as sending an email. For others it'll be something to learn as they go, and for some it'll be something they never quite get their heads around.

The switch to remote working hasn't created a problem with digital literacy. But it has highlighted a problem that's been around for a while. The World Economic Forum published a report in 2020 entitled *Accelerating Digital Inclusion in the New Normal* that examined the causes of and solutions to what it described as an absence of adoption and maturity of basic digital literacy practices. In a nutshell, most of us need some digital literacy training if we want to succeed within a distributed workforce.

Offices are good places to be if your digital literacy is low. There's usually someone around to help you out. Under the remote model, you're pretty much on your own. When we say digital literacy, what we mean in the context of remote or hybrid working is having a basic understanding of and competence with the tools that were once useful, but are now essential. So in practice that means the ability to attach a file to an email or edit a spreadsheet.

The lack of digital literacy within some sectors has been a barrier to progress for organizations trying to go remote. The problem is far more pronounced in smaller businesses, perhaps because they lack the resources to enact sufficient training. In fact, according to the World Economic Forum report, 'at most, 10–20 per cent of SME employees have been able to work remotely during lockdowns versus over 50 per cent for large companies, even in high income markets such as Japan'.

The report, conducted in partnership with Boston Consulting Group, laid out some pretty stark facts for anyone doubting the claim that digital literacy is pretty low across the board. Businesses, specifically small and medium-sized enterprises (SMEs), have been lagging behind and are particularly exposed in this crisis, despite the critical role they play in global economies. SMEs represent more than 90 per cent of businesses worldwide and half of global employment, and even more in emerging markets where they drive more than half of gross domestic product (GDP). However they lag far behind larger companies in terms of information communications technology (ICT) adoption and maturity. Less than half have fixed broadband connectivity and overall less than a quarter are digitized (offering some service online) compared to almost 100 per cent for larger companies.'

Employers need to respond to this and do it quickly. A computer problem in the context of an office is inconvenient for as long as it takes IT support to fix it. A computer problem in a remote context can be isolating and anxiety inducing.

Dealing with digital presenteeism

In October 2021 the *Telegraph* published an article about colds. Alice Hall, a feature writer covering health and wellness topics, had noticed social media users complaining in significant numbers about an experience they were describing as being like 'the worst cold ever'. 'In the pre-pandemic world, colds weren't something to be taken seriously,' Hall noted: 'it was quite common to suffer through a day's work while blowing into a hanky or attend a meeting with streaming eyes. But anecdotally, simply getting through a day's work with the super cold is near impossible' (Hall and Rowan, 2021).

Hall, like many others, suspected the surge in 'super-sniffles' was due to widely adopted Covid-19 avoidance habits, such as improved hand hygiene and mask wearing, leading to an increase in our susceptibility to other bugs. The experts agreed. According to Professor Ronald Eccles, Emeritus Professor at Cardiff University and former director of the Common Cold Centre, our immune systems simply weren't on guard for the common cold because we'd been protecting them from Covid-19. 'Normally, we are exposed to these viruses on a daily or weekly basis. But now we're like athletes out of condition who haven't trained for a year. We've suddenly got this virus and our immune system is overreacting to it,' he explained (Hall and Rowan, 2021).

If you read Hall's own summary back to yourself, there's something quite telling, and depressing. It has traditionally been common for us to 'suffer' through a day's work when ill. And, of course, that should never have been the case. There's a bit of irony here. Covid-19 has of course been the main driver behind our shift to working from home. And it is now the reason we seemingly can't fight off a common cold. Employers and policy makers should be taking note.

To borrow a popular pandemic-time phrase from the UK government, remote working has given us a precious opportunity for a 'circuit break'. If we can't take this opportunity now to re-evaluate the relationship between work and health, specifically our habit for presenteeism, we'll probably never do it. As it relates to being 'at work', we can crudely split our state of (ill) health at any time into two categories: 'too ill to come into the office'; and 'too ill to work'.

In the past, unhealthy workplace cultures predicated on encouraging presenteeism have incentivized many of us to ignore signs from each category; before the Covid-19 pandemic, workers would routinely attend the office when they should have been working from home to protect their colleagues and – far worse – workers would routinely work when they were simply too unwell to do so. Remote working presents many opportunities for improved productivity, but there's a risk here that having employees away from the office will increase, not decrease, the number of people working when they should be in bed. We must strive to avoid at all costs a blurring of the lines between 'too ill to come in' and 'too ill to work'. Employers need to start thinking very carefully about how they sensitively, and without intrusion, monitor and record the health of their employees so that they aren't tempted into working from home when they should be convalescing. There are countless reasons why this should be a priority for organizations leaning in to remote work culture. Not least because working while ill is bad for ill people and it's bad for business.

The UK government already has a definition for 'digital presenteeism'. 'Digital presenteeism is when you feel under pressure to always be available online, via video calls, phone, email, chat or Slack. It's when you've done a full day's work, but feel pressure to log on or reply later than your normal or preferred working patterns, even if you feel exhausted or unwell' (Peel, 2020). Whatever its many faults, the UK government has some good advice on tackling digital presenteeism. It advises workers and employers to adopt an approach focused around honesty, boundaries and expectation setting, with a recommendation that workers 'agree to be absent', saying, 'if you are not adding value to a meeting or not getting anything out of it, decline it or duck out early. You can give that time back for yourself' (Peel, 2020).

While this is genuinely good advice, we needn't get carried away heaping praise on the source of this advice. It's easy for a government to publish advice to workers on what they can do for themselves to improve their own workplace wellness. It's much harder for a government to enact policies that ensure workers will be listened to and treated fairly should they actually try to take that advice. According to Office for National Statistics data released in September 2021, the UK has 29.1 million payroll employees. Those 29.1 million people are entitled to ask for more than a blog post with recommendations, as solid as those recommendations might be. This book is probably not the place for examining governmental shortcomings in regard to workplace wellness policy, sick pay and employment regulations, but it's safe to say the mixed messages and U-turns on whether we should be working from home, working from an office or working at all haven't necessarily helped empower workers to pursue and prioritize their own wellness in the workplace. That said, 'agree to be absent' isn't a bad bit of shorthand for what we should be discussing. So let's go with it.

Presenteeism is bad for workers, bad for businesses and bad for economies. It always has been. According to a 2016 report by Pathology Awareness Australia (PAA), 'sick workers dragging themselves into the office are costing the Australian economy more than $34 billion a year' (Carter, 2016). John Crothers, Chair of PAA, said of the report's findings that presenteeism is 'all about not understanding what's going on with their healthcare at that point in time'. Crothers summarized the mental state underpinning our instinct for presenteeism quite neatly. 'Yes, you've got a deadline to hit – but you want to do that in the understanding that your body's in a position to be able to do that effectively, and not underperforming and not spreading something that might actually be contagious.'

We're at a crossroads. There's an opportunity to weave the idea of 'agreeing to be absent' into remote work culture and hybrid culture. A worker with a mild cold who genuinely feels they can get things done without damaging their own health should work from home. That way, they can remain productive, avoid the stress of having to catch up on what they've missed, but – crucially – not pass on whatever they've got to their colleagues. There's also a huge, conflicting temptation for employers to allow their workers to be digitally present when they should be physically (and digitally absent). Employees who may ordinarily have phoned in sick, possibly empowered to do so by hard-to-ignore physical symptoms, may be unable to resist the temptation to struggle away from their sofa. For all of the physical cues the office provides us about when and how to work, it's going to be hard for employees to get past the idea that if they can sit up straight on their sofa at home, they should be working. It's going to be harder still for employers to prevent them from doing so.

The UK government's blog we cited earlier offers a potential model for combatting this. 'Establish a "wellbeing team charter" for how your team behaves. Set the expectation for others too for what is acceptable and what isn't. This goes for more senior people too!' (Peel, 2020). Combatting presenteeism is all about leadership and expectation setting. Junior employees need to see their workplace leaders setting standards of self-care that they can comfortably emulate and adopt. Organizations should be strict with enforcing an anti-presenteeism culture. Managers coughing their way through conference calls or logging into Zoom calls with a runny nose will be the reason organizations fail in tackling this. Junior employers and even senior employers with less self-confidence to lead will see workplace leaders struggling through the day and perceive that to be the expected standard. So we need brave corporate leaders who can embrace and visibly take ownership of their own wellbeing combined with frameworks and policies that go further than simply discouraging this sort of behaviour and actively penalize it with disciplinary measures. Informal steps will be important too. Organizations should encourage their leaders to be open about taking ownership of their wellness. The impact of a well-regarded boss emailing his or her team to say they are taking the day off to recover from a cold cannot be understated. At the very least, organizations need to strive for a culture that doesn't glorify any sort of self-defeating, unhealthy behaviour, and they should be aiming to establish concrete steps that stamp it out. As with discouraging over-work, there's a big difference between saying 'We *don't expect* you to work if you're not well' and 'We *expect you not* to work if you're not well.'

Richard Howard is a Director at a legal services company in Nottingham. He explained in an interview with us that he and his fellow directors had developed a policy of 'spot checking' colleagues to monitor their wellness. 'As a group of directors we tried to vary how we contacted our staff,' he explained. 'We made arrangements together to set aside time where we would call staff in other departments, out of the blue, just to ask how they are. We occasionally picked people we were concerned about too. We felt we got more honesty by using a different voice, and the unexpected nature of the call meant we got unprepared answers. It led to some good chats, and we made several changes off the back of these chats to make staff feel more included in the group, or give them access to something they were missing.'

Zorica, the SEO specialist we mentioned previously who works for a global money transfer platform, is one of the many thousands of people who've experienced remote working in the past. She has brought her existing skill and knowledge of the dynamics and challenges of remote working into her current permanent role. 'I used to freelance and work for companies that were fully remote before joining my current place, so switching to remote working didn't take a lot of adjusting for me. Using tools such as Zoom, Google Docs and Slack was already a part of my daily routine. Most of my team members are in Budapest, Tallinn and London so we are more or less aligned when it comes to time zones, which is helpful.

In 2021 her employer switched to a hybrid approach that includes a generous annual allowance for working from anywhere. 'Working here gives me an opportunity to get the best of both worlds, to enjoy the flexibility of working from anywhere but also to meet and collaborate with my colleagues in person. And this is definitely one of my favourite things about where I work. I definitely plan to use the allowance to visit family and friends back home but also to explore and spend some time in other countries.

'Besides the annual "work from anywhere" allowance, we can also work from home up to three days a week which really gives us a lot of flexibility. As I had fully remote work experience in the past, I can say that this hybrid approach works really well for me. I enjoy both.'

Her employer has enacted some relatively bold steps in their embrace of hybrid working that have clear and obvious benefits for all employees that want to take advantage. But Zorica has noticed more subtle improvements that feed back into her ability to work to the peak of her powers. 'My work–life balance has improved greatly in some ways. Since commuting is eliminated from my daily routine I use this extra time to exercise or focus on hobbies and meeting friends. The change of scenery and the ability to travel and spend time working abroad also had a positive effect on my productivity and motivation. The biggest perk is simply having more energy and more time to do things that matter.'

Like many organizations, Zorica's company has remotely onboarded a number of new team members. Zorica couldn't help but be impressed with how management found ways to remotely build a sense of belonging for new and existing staff. 'The company did a couple of great things to get us onboarded faster to remote working. It was very useful to hear about all the wonderful communities we have right from the very beginning. For instance, we have a Slack channel which is a safe space for people who identify as women. We also have Slack communities for black employees, queer employees, parents and carers and many others as well.

'Since the pandemic prevented us from meeting in person my team came up with an interesting idea of organizing virtual coffee chats. Newbies were paired in groups of three or four people so they had an opportunity to meet other people in the team.'

Responding to failure

It's not a nice thing to admit, but some workers will be exposed by the switch to remote. Workers who previously concealed their on-the-job weaknesses with their gregarious personality, diplomatic nature or just by being very likeable are going to find that those good qualities – and they are good qualities – are not enough to get by anymore.

Mediocre workers that were nice to be around are going to stick out like a sore thumb. It's important to clarify at this point that we are not advocating for employers to treat each worker as a source of productivity outputs and nothing else. Soft skills are essential to team building and management. But certain workers will find that without in-person contact, they find it harder to conceal their work-related shortcomings. Organizations must resist at all costs adopting a culture of dehumanization. Lack of contact and lack of proximity will make it very convenient to judge workers solely on their contribution to the bottom line. In fact, some of the staunchest advocates for remote work see this as one of the major benefits of remote working. These people could ruin it for the rest of us.

In Chapter 2 we discussed performance monitoring and cutting out 'noise', such as apparent busyness, from how we evaluate worker effectiveness. This does not mean employers should judge every employee solely on their metrics. If that was the right way to do things, we'd have already been doing it. Writing in *The Atlantic*, CEO of PR firm EZPR Ed Zitron argues that 'workers are happier because they don't have to commute and can be evaluated mostly on their actual work rather than on the optics-driven albatross of "office culture"' (Zitron, 2021). Ed is correct in some ways, but in our view he should have stated that *some* workers were happier. Lots of workers will be harbouring anxieties about being 'found out', because remote working, for better or worse, doesn't provide them with a sufficiently well-attended arena in which to be seen to be adding value.

This scenario is a failure of management as much as a failure on the part of the worker. In fact, it's not improbable that those most exposed by remote working will actually be management. The data driven approach we looked at in Chapter 2 has the potential to drive lots of efficiencies and bring out the best in some employees. But it doesn't take a data analyst to spot a bad worker. Their performance data will most likely accord with people's rapidly formed and strongly held opinions of them. Genuinely bad workers have a habit of advertising themselves quite clearly. It's not the bad hires that we're actually talking about here. The people who will have their flaws most painfully exposed by remote work are those who underperform but still add some degree of value. To lean on the footballer analogy once more, these workers have a lot of the hallmarks of a 20-goal-a-season striker, but their stats don't back it up.

The reason we're talking about this here is because responding to the needs of this type of worker is very much a wellbeing consideration and very much not a productivity matter.

Inclusion

There are two significant cultural faced by companies who make the permanent switch to distributed or hybrid work forces. First, they risk installing hierarchies based on location. Second, they risk creating tensions between those who come into the office and those who do not.

For organizations reluctant to embrace remote work, one of the most compelling arguments in favour of it is that most organizations, even the ones who are publicly against the idea, have actually been doing it for years. There are very few businesses that manage every aspect of their operations in-house.

Google has almost 140,000 employees across approximately 70 sites around the world. It has invested billions in its offices. In 2017 Google finalized plans for an impressive £1 billion site in London's King's Cross. Designed to house 4,000 employees and with a swimming pool, massage rooms and a rooftop garden, you might wonder why anyone with access to such a workplace would ever want to leave it, let alone work from home. When it comes to comfort and perks, Google's famous campuses are the benchmark. Despite most of its staff working remotely during the pandemic, the tech giant resumed construction in mid-2020 (Partridge, 2020) after a pause during lockdown, reaffirming its commitment to the giant hub.

Of all the companies on earth that would need outside support, you wouldn't think it'd be Google. Yet in 2018 Bloomberg reported that the tech behemoth was operating with a 'shadow workforce' of contractors that can represent up to half of its total headcount, depending on demand. In 2018, Google's non-permanent staff outnumbered direct employees for the first time (Bergen and Eidelson, 2018).

Why would a company like Google, famously committed to creating great working environments and supportive work culture, have half of its workforce outside of the organization? It's partially an accounting trick. 'Investors watch employee headcount closely at these tech powerhouses, expecting that they keep posting impressive gains by maintaining skinnier workforces than older corporate titans,' explain Bergen and Eidelson in their report. It's also because even companies like Google don't have all the resources they need, all of the time. They need outside help.

So Google's motivation is clear. Outside contractors are handy for peaks in demand and give the impression of a lean headcount. But why would those workers want to meet the mental demands of working for Google without access to its famous perks package? Well, in many cases, they're not happy about it and would prefer to be employed directly. The Bloomberg report revealed that many of Google's contractors felt like an 'underclass'. And that highlights one of the big risks of pivoting to a remote-first model. It can breed inequality, and that is something this book will examine in more detail in Chapter 9.

Achieving belonging

As David Heinemeier Hansson and Jason Fried point out in their 2013 book *Remote: Office not required*, businesses outsource things like legal services, accountancy, advertising and public relations every day, with very little inconvenience. And there's plenty that reluctant managers can take from the outsourcing model to help them deal with their reluctance to permit remote work for employees.

Many of the companies that built tools to facilitate our switch to remote work are themselves staffed by remote workers. Basecamp for project management, Slack for internal communications, GitHub for code storage and review, Google and Microsoft for everything else – all of these companies have spoken publicly about the benefits of remote work. In the case of GitHub, which relies on an army of contributors around the world to underpin its open-source model, it's doubtful it would exist without remote work.

Remote: Office not required was written long before most of us held any notion of a mass shift to remote work. And, for that reason, there's something fundamentally more pure about the things for which the authors advocate. They're not approaching remote work as an inevitability, something out of their control that needs to be managed. Theirs is much more of an holistic approach to embracing the liberalizing elements of remote work while retaining as many of the benefits of office culture as possible. One thing the authors strongly support is the idea of remote inclusion. They recommend organizations strive to create a 'virtual water cooler', a place where their team can bring their 'whole selves' to work. 'We all need mindless breaks, and it helps if you spend some of them with your team. That's where the virtual water cooler comes in,' they explain. 'We use a chat program we created called Campfire. Other techy shops use IRC servers to achieve the same. The idea is to have a single, permanent chat room where everyone hangs out all day to shoot the breeze, post funny pictures, and generally goof around. Yes, it can also be used to answer questions about work, but its primary function is to provide social cohesion' (Heinemeier Hansson and Fried, 2013).

The authors are both software developers and their most famous product is the remote collaboration tool Basecamp. They are in the business of building software products to solve their own problems. And they started writing their book in 2013, the same year Slack was launched. If they'd written the book today they'd most likely have cited Slack and its alternatives, such as Monday.com, Microsoft Teams and Webex as worthy alternatives.

One advantage, Heinemeier Hansson and Fried claim, to virtual water coolers is that the remote worker gets to govern just how much interaction they get involved with. This means that you, the remote worker, are in control of your social interaction – when it happens and how much of it you need. 'At first it might simply seem like a waste of time, especially if you're not already used to reading Reddit on the side, but it's a quality waste of time with your co-workers. We all need that.'

07

Remote by design

A case study

Sean has spent the vast majority of his career working remotely, and has run a remote-first business since 2015. In this chapter he outlines the various unpublicised benefits, demystifies some of the myths around remote working culture and explains how his businesses embraces remoteness to create a culture of autonomy.

The theme tune to the BBC's *Antiques Roadshow* can still make my stomach turn. I have nothing against the programme whatsoever, but ever since childhood its jaunty melody served as an audible cue that that Sunday afternoon, and therefore the weekend, was coming to an end. In my school days, *Antiques Roadshow* was the gateway back into the school week. I resented being reminded that I had homework left to do, a school bag to pack and – most importantly – I had to get my brain in gear for the coming week.

Unfortunately for me, *Antiques Roadshow* induced nausea persisted into adulthood. For an unacceptably long period of time in my adult life, approximately 50 per cent of every weekend was spent dreading the following morning, with the dread intensifying from as early as Saturday night, but always peaking just after dinner time on Sunday. There was a period of about seven years which started with university and ended abruptly after a four-year period of insecure freelancing from home where Sundays were tolerable in their entirety because there was no school, no commute and no office to get to the next day. But for the rest of the time between then and 2015 I spent half my weekends worrying about the day to come. The Sunday evening nausea intensified during a period in my life when I decided that freelancing was too unpredictable and that I should probably get a proper job.

The first 'proper job' was editing a consumer affairs website, and it was actually fine in retrospect, but having that job, in an office, still ruined my Sundays. My boss was very hands-off, my colleagues were fun and the work was interesting. I fell into a false sense of security and then I got cocky and decided I wanted to own my own home. So I took what a recruitment consultant called a 'logical next step' in my career and moved to a job with better pay, more benefits, more responsibility and – unfortunately for me – a CEO with genuine psychopathic tendencies. On the second day of that job I rang the recruitment consultant and asked him to help me find a job without a psychopathic CEO at the helm. Mere weeks later I was out of there and working at an ostensibly 'fun' and 'dynamic' creative agency. It was the polar opposite of the toxic environment I'd sleepwalked into, but it was still toxic in its own way. Instead of wearing a suit and living in fear of the company founder stopping me in the corridor and asking me to recite the seven pillars of the business' culture, I wore jeans and lived in fear of the company founder stopping me in a corridor and attempting to converse with me in any way, such was the appeal of his personality to me at the time. That role lasted slightly longer than the previous one but ended in a similar fashion, the week before Christmas. It was at that point that I decided I couldn't ever again have a proper job in a proper office and would go back to freelancing, but do it properly this time.

For years, Essential Content was just an email address, a website holding page and a Google Chromebook that cost £199. This was, and probably would still be, entirely sufficient for me to operate my business. Essential Content was what might now be called a 'side hustle' that kept me sane during the four-year period working in-house and agency side in a handful of unfulfilling and mentally ruinous office-based roles. Having an assortment of badly paying freelance jobs on the side, which I did in the mornings before leaving for various offices, kept me sane because it felt like an escape plan if I needed it. And thankfully this small source of additional income, more often than not received via PayPal, was a lifeline when I decided I did need to escape the world of 'proper jobs'. Having discussed it with various qualified professionals since, my aversion to proper jobs, discomfort in offices and genuine fear of one day having to go and get one again is not rooted in laziness but in my own (in)ability to tolerate authority figures. I once had an anxiety attack when a line manager forgot to approve a holiday request and I had to send the 'just chasing this one up' email.

The Essential Content email I set up is still my email address, and it's all I have needed to earn a living as a freelance writer and publicist for years. But in 2015 a potential client explained to me that they couldn't hire me unless I was incorporated, for insurance and compliance reasons. (Ironically, that same client today would be legally unable to hire me on the same terms due to IR35 regulations.) So I emailed my brother and asked him how to set up a limited company. It was significantly easier than I expected. There are companies offering 'off-the-shelf' limited companies and this is a really handy way to do it. They will have a number of registered entities, with company numbers, articles of association and all the other official things you need to legally incorporate a company. All you have to do is come up with a name and pay a relatively small registration fee. Speaking of the fee, these organizations can afford to charge a relatively low fee for what is quite a comprehensive service because they make their money once you're up and running by selling your data to all sorts of third parties who would have an interest in selling services to newly incorporated businesses. So if you do ever set up a limited company and this is the route you take, be prepared to be spammed.

For the first two years of its life, Essential Content Ltd was still little more than an administrative concept, a legal entity through which to invoice, pay bills and hold the relevant business insurances required by clients. It was a corporate wrapper with a brand identity designed by someone in Vietnam whom I'd never met. But it was an unexpected catalyst. Having annual accounts, statements of confirmation, corporation tax and all the other really fun stuff associated with running a 'proper' business made me think that I should probably start taking myself a little more seriously. So I used that identity to project something approaching a business image that potential clients could put their trust in. I was genuinely amazed by how much more seriously people took me as a company director compared to when I was 'just' a freelancer, even though the only thing that had changed was the legal structure I was operating in and the kind of taxes I paid. Incorporating the businesses didn't mean I suddenly had lots of staff, big offices or shareholders (apart from myself).

So the wrapper of Essential Content was extremely useful for one big reason; it helped me transition from being a freelancer, through the awkward grey space of 'freelancer working with others' into what is now a small agency. For a large portion of those first two years, Essential Content was just me with occasional administrative support from a virtual assistant based in the Philippines. This isn't faux humility to downplay what the business is today, those first two years produced a body of work I'm very proud of on behalf of a number of household name clients including the BBC, Co-operative Bank and TransferWise. It's important to be clear about the ease with which a very small business can project an image of being larger and more prestigious than it actually is. And as long as the work is delivered on time, in budget and to the standard expected, it actually doesn't matter.

Essential Content as a business could not have survived without remote work. At the time of its founding I was emotionally incapable of taking on any work that required my physical presence in a set location. So I could only work with clients that were comfortable with having suppliers who were remote. Thankfully, copywriting and public relations are two types of work that I think have been ahead of the curve for years in regard to location independence. They're a bit like accountancy, graphic design and a range of other disciplines that for some reason are just assumed to be easily outsource-able.

Looking back, it's now possible to be a bit more relaxed about what were very humble beginnings. There were moments when it felt like the scene in *The Wizard of Oz* when the wizard tells Dorothy 'pay no attention to that man behind the curtain' with me being both the man behind the curtain and the man telling others not to pay attention to him. Had clients taken a peek to see me working until 2 am and using email scheduling tool Boomerang to send the work over at a professionally acceptable time like 8.11 am the following morning while I was asleep (always send scheduled emails at 'odd' times, so it looks more natural; never use the default half-hourly units), they might have doubted their own faith in me.

Outwardly, the 'headquarters' for the first two years were impressive; an address in the same cluster of buildings as the BBC, ITV, Barclays Bank, Reckitt Benckiser and a number of exciting AI, tech and new media startups. Inwardly, the reality was less prestigious. Essential Content's actual headquarters was any available desk in a co-working space. But it didn't matter because all Essential Content actually needed to operate was a desk, a chair and reliable WiFi.

The business has now matured and has many of the characteristics you might associate with a 'proper' company: a head office, a workforce, a proper website, a LinkedIn profile, online reviews, an accountant and an expired company debit card which I've kept because I genuinely didn't believe the business would last longer than the expiry date on the first company debit card. But it is, has always been and will always be remote by design. According to data from the US Bureau of Labor Statistics, approximately 20 per cent of small businesses in America 'fail within the first year' (Carter, 2021). Year 2 is worse, as '30 percent of businesses will have failed. By the end of the fifth year, about half will have failed' (Carter, 2021). In the UK, the survival rate for new businesses is even worse. According to the Office for National Statistics, roughly 80 per cent of UK companies fail within their first year (Scottish Financial News, 2020).

Remoteness is the only reason Essential Content made it through the risky first two years. More specifically, Essential Content is still alive today because it doesn't have a 'proper office' and the associated overheads and it isn't constrained by geography when it comes to recruitment. The lack of office overhead has meant that we've been able to compete for work against more established businesses who have no choice but to bake their fixed costs into their fees. And I've had more than one client tell us they're happy that we don't have large, expensive offices, because they don't like the idea of paying for it. By far the most important benefit of being a remote by design business has been the ability to hire from outside of our immediate geography (or persuade people to move to be nearer to the mythical headquarters). We've consistently hired the people best suited to help us deliver what we need, with some caveats. Essential Content has had to compete with larger, richer and more established businesses for talent. So we've been turned down numerous times by people who are put off by the absence of an office because understandably they treat the presence of an office as a signifier of legitimacy.

That said, we've benefited more from remoteness than we've suffered. In the six years (at time of writing) since Essential Content was incorporated, we've hired talented people from Blackburn, Belfast, London, Durham, Dallas, Ho Chi Minh City, Nottingham and of course from our own neighbourhood of Greater Manchester. In fact, one quirk of being remote first is that Manchester is home to two of Essential Content's longest serving people and even accounting for almost two years of Covid-19 enforced isolation, these are the two people we have the least contact with. In one case, this is entirely deliberate; her entire work ethic is based on not speaking to clients, being invited to conference calls or otherwise interrupted from doing what she does best, which is writing exceptionally deep and detailed articles.

Challenges

There's an ironic twist to being the founder of a remote first business, writing a book about remote work, at a time when more and more businesses are pivoting to a distributed workforce. It means that one of our biggest recruitment advantages has been taken away. The fact that you could work for Essential Content and live anywhere in the world was, until last year, both a novelty and – for the profile of worker we are attracted to – an enormous sell. While it's hopefully not the only reason we've been able to attract talented people to our businesses, it's the only factor that has ever broken the deadlock when a candidate was considering another offer. We once secured the services of a busy and in-demand publicist because she'd recently got a new dog and wanted to work from home so she could house train her pup without losing income. Historically, it's been almost impossible, all other things being equal, to compete with the idea that you can work for what is now an established communications agency and literally work wherever you fancy, doing the hours that best suit your lifestyle.

Culture: An antisocial, family-first business

Due to the absence of a centralized office, Essential Content hasn't really got what you'd describe as a traditional workplace culture. It has none of the things that you might consider to characterize a work culture. There is zero scope for off-the-cuff 'water cooler moments', there are no after-work drinks – or anything social, for that matter. We tried to organize team Christmas dinners a few years on the bounce but with the travel required from a distributed workforce we could never align enough diaries to make it worthwhile. So we've since given up on that. In fact, you could reasonably describe our culture as 'antisocial'. If you've ever begrudged the need to 'show your face' at a work social event, you might enjoy working with us because there aren't any. Our policy regarding social events is that they're best spent with the people you've chosen to build your life around, such as friends and family. The fear is that if we start trying to organize Christmas parties or social get-togethers, people will feel obliged to attend when they could be doing something genuinely fun. There is a ceiling to the amount of fun you can have in the presence of people who you work with. The organization of our company doesn't lend itself particularly well to the forming of workplace friendships, so why try to force it?

In fact, there are certain people within our organization that have never spoken to each other. This is in no way unusual for large companies, but at its maximum Essential Content retains the services of no more than 20 individuals. In a bricks and mortar context, good manners and chance dictate that after a period of no more than six months everyone would have met. It isn't exactly a deliberate policy, but we see little value in forcing introductions between people working in different time zones, on different projects, who will have no professional interaction at all.

What culture the business does have is informed by the nature of the work we do, the types of clients we work with and the fact that the entire workforce is distributed, even those in Manchester. By necessity, Essential Content has developed a culture that could best be described as 'get the work done then do something more important'. One member of our team described it as a 'family-first culture', which is not far off the mark. We are open and accepting of the fact that, in many cases, people would rather be spending time with their loved ones than working. We work with that reality, not against it, and have no problem with people finding solutions that enable them to maximize the amount of time they spend away from their computers.

Having reflected on it for a long time, if that's the culture then it is not part of some grand altruistic gesture, but rather an outcome of the fact that the business processes and procedures lend themselves well to flexibility. One of the reasons we function well as a business is that the vast majority of people have very specifically defined deliverables. These aren't key performance indicators. They are specific, measurable tasks that, once complete, should theoretically require no further involvement. So there's a huge incentive for efficiency from members of our team to get their work done as quickly as they can so they can spend the rest of the day doing something important, like being with their family or friends. We have a number of informal policies to facilitate this, including:

Minimal ad hoc tasks

Ad hoc tasks are an absolute spanner in the works if you're relying on people you work with working deeply and with focus. We try to limit these where possible and always try to bundle smaller jobs into larger packages of work to which we can attach measurable progress.

No fixed hours

This applies to the vast majority of people we work with. Instead of setting hours and billing accordingly, everyone who works with us has a clear understanding of their deliverables. Once they've delivered their deliverables, it's none of our business how they spend their time.

Centralized workflow

We use Google Drive for almost everything, so nobody ever has to send an email asking for a document. Google Drive works well because its built-in features mirror the sort of processes we use. For example, its version history function lets us review changes made by different document collaborators. With Google Drive, we're really careful to limit permissions both for confidentiality reasons and to prevent people having access to documents that are of no relevance.

Outsourcing allowed

Our freelancers are perfectly entitled to outsource or subcontract parts of their work if they need to. Provided the quality and style remains the same (and they provide us with signed non-disclosure agreements and completed risk assessments), we have no strong opinion on who actually created it. The only stipulations we have on this policy are that we only deal with the freelancer we hired and that we are unable to tell the difference between work they produced themselves, and work they outsourced. This is probably the most eyebrow-raising habit we've adopted because it implies that we are giving away control of the work. The truth is, outsourcing saves us an enormous amount of trouble and allows us to scale much more effectively. We only decided to implement this policy when one of our freelancers revealed that she was anxious because she felt she was hitting her capacity with us, but didn't want to seem ungrateful. If we could have cloned her, we would have. We were faced with the challenge of having to find another freelancer with a very similar set of skills to share some of the workload. That would have involved training and onboarding. So the next best thing to cloning was entrusting her to share her workload with people she could train herself, who she trusted. This enabled her to expand her capacity without over-committing her time. She was able to manage the workflow, ensure consistent quality and, to be frank, was by far the best placed person to take ownership of this process because she was the subject matter expert and that's why we hired her.

A modular workforce

To better understand how and why the business lends itself well to remote work, it's worth briefly explaining the kind of work we do. Essential Content is a communications agency specializing in two specific types of communication: public relations and user experience. Public relations involves managing our clients' external reputations. This involves a blend of activities ranging from writing press releases to arranging TV interviews. Approximately 50 per cent of the work involved in PR – the way we do it anyway – is written. Thirty per cent of the work is research-based and analytical, for example monitoring brand mentions, researching stories and reacting to news. Twenty per cent is interpersonal, for example 'selling in' a PR campaign to journalists. This element is done by email and over the phone. None of it is done in person.

User experience and the related field of content design involve improving and measuring how our clients' customers and service users are able to interact with their products and services. For example, one day we might be working on the wording for a web page to help a user reset their password. The following day we might be writing content that guides a user through the process of making a car insurance claim online or via an app or composing a letter that explains to a customer that they've been declined or accepted for a mortgage. It's a good mix of activity but it's all communication based.

Every person delivering work for Essential Content, apart from myself, is freelance. This is deliberate and it isn't determined by cost. In fact, the business probably pays slightly more on the whole for staff than it would do for the equivalent number of hours from full-time, permanent staff. This approach isn't suitable for every business and there may come a time when it's appropriate to either offer full-time positions to the freelancers working for us (whether they'd want them is another matter) or to start advertising full-time permanent roles. But for now, our workforce of approximately 17 freelance specialists is precisely what the business needs to serve our clients.

There are multiple advantages to working in this way. The main advantage is the flexibility it affords. Without a fixed staff overhead, we can assemble specialist teams for each project. It's possible that we can scale down the work we offer each freelancer, but it rarely happens. We do often scale up the work though.

We have an informal 'non-exclusivity' rule that demands Essential Content should represent no more than 40 per cent of total work time for any one freelancer, regardless of what they do. We have a strong preference for freelancers for whom the other 60 or more per cent of work is split across at least two other clients. But that is just a preference, and frankly it's none of our business what people do when they're not working for us. The point is that if Essential Content is a freelancer's sole or predominant source of income, there are implications for their tax status; and also it suggests that this particular freelancer doesn't have much else going on. Sometimes we have to break that rule and temporarily scale up a freelancer's workload, which affects their ratios, but on the whole we endeavour to make sure that we only use freelancers who have a healthy pipeline of other client work.

This is useful for two reasons. The first has to do with imposter syndrome. Eventually the feeling may disappear, but since day one I've been working on the assumption that at some point I would be 'found out' and all of our clients would abandon us. I live in a fairly constant state of low-level anxiety about getting tapped on the shoulder and told 'The game is up!' It's why I was so surprised to see the businesses outlive the first debit card. Enduring that situation, or anything close to it, while having freelancers for whom Essential Content represents anything more than 50 per cent of their entire workload would be heart-breaking. It helps me sleep better at night knowing that, if anything disastrous happened to the business – for example a global pandemic that disrupted every industry our clients operate in – everyone who works for us would (theoretically) have other income streams to keep them afloat.

The second and more important reason why this 40–60 approach is useful for us has to do with what we gain when our freelancers are working for other clients. We share freelancers with a lot of brilliant organizations, ranging in size from community-owned street markets and startups to massive, historical, household brand names. Freelancers who work for Essential Content also work for or have worked for the following organizations; Which?, Kelloggs, ITV, Virgin Group, Barclays Bank, Mediacom, Weber Shandwick, Disney, Nike, Autotrader and many others. We feel that when it comes to talent, we punch significantly above our weight. In terms of revenue or reputation, Essential Content isn't even a blip on the radar of these organizations. Yet we are able to hire the same calibre of people – literally the same people – they do for the same price, sometimes less, albeit in smaller volumes. The only reason we are able to attract the sorts of freelancers that have work offers from the companies named above is that we've traditionally been able to offer them something that their other clients could not – complete and total location independence, and a significant increase in autonomy. I'll explain more about this later in this case study.

This approach means that the level of expertise and quality of experience at our disposal is exceptional. The value we gain as a business from the insights of our freelancers is hard to measure, but it's huge. The means by which we capture this knowledge and insight varies, but here's one scenario where the knowledge a freelancer has picked up working for another client has directly benefited us.

Essential Content was developing a strategy for a consumer public relations campaign. In Slack, we were discussing the idea of offering the finished story as an exclusive to the Press Association. We were also discussing the idea of commissioning a consumer poll to generate data to back up our story. One of our media relations freelancers, who wasn't even working on this project, messaged on WhatsApp in the evening to say she'd read the Slack conversation on her phone and that she strongly advised against spending client budget on a poll if the Press Association was our target platform. She made this recommendation because one of her other clients had recently given up doing exactly what we were planning to do, because the Press Association simply 'have really gone off poll content'. The opportunity cost of offering an exclusive to the Press Association is huge. While you're waiting for a response, you can't offer the same story to another publisher because it would no longer be an exclusive by definition. That opportunity cost increases by orders of magnitude when, without knowing it, you're planning to offer them something in a format they are unlikely to want. Then there's the actual cost of the polling. In this case we were planning to spend approximately £2,000 to get the data we thought the story required. The freelancer recommended that we went ahead with the polling, but kept it separate from the content we offered to the Press Association. She also mentioned that she had a contact at the Press Association who may be interested in our story, but that they didn't work on Mondays or Tuesdays, so if we were prepared to wait until the following week, she'd be able to speak to them.

This somewhat loose and informal method of insight sharing is significantly less likely to occur in a scenario where everyone who works for you does so exclusively. Where would they pick it up from? The only comparable situation I can think of is when a company makes a new hire from a competitor and they 'brain dump' everything they know about that competitor in their first week.

Job splitting

Another exceptional benefit of working with freelancers is that you can easily split projects between two people. Why pay one person for eight days' worth of work when you can pay two people for four days' worth of work while getting double the experience, double the perspective, and double the insight delivered in half the time for the same price? Getting a second pair of eyes on an idea or a piece of work confers an immeasurable amount of intangible benefit. There's something about the cooperation, friction and competition that happens when you've got two people collaborating vs one person on a solo project. It's not always appropriate or useful to do it this way but the flexibility to treat any given project as a 'job share' without any HR involvement at all has benefited the business and its clients.

Specific deliverables vs time tracking

Another important ingredient in the mix is that we mainly work to very specific and defined goals, project by project. People have a very clear sense of when their work is done and the business has a very clear sense of what is being delivered. This means that there is no obligation on any freelancer to kill time on the clock, as you would do in a traditional office environment.

The vast majority, approximately 70 per cent, of people working inside the business produce written content. On the public relations side that can be any of the following things; thought leadership articles, press releases, white papers, spokespeople quotes, media briefing documents and journalist pitches. On the user experience side of our business, that can be wireframes (a sort of web page prototype), high fidelity prototypes in shared software like Figma, scamps (low fidelity prototypes), user journey flow diagrams, error messages, banner copy and terms and conditions. As with the PR content, these are finite tasks with a defined endpoint. If we need revisions or additions, in most cases we brief these separately and pay additionally to have them done. Some of our suppliers charge us based on the assumption that we will require a certain amount of revisions and they bake that into their price.

Writing work lends itself well to having a distributed workforce. We're under no illusions that this model can't necessarily be replicated identically in other contexts. It simply won't work for certain types of work. But for the types of work we deliver, and I believe for a variety of other types of work, remoteness isn't just a compromise, it's the optimum way of running the business.

Measuring success in a distributed workforce

Our way of measuring success is atypical, and would certainly not work in all scenarios. We've covered more general methods of measuring success in Chapter 2, so what follows is an explanation of how we measure success as a business in order to provide context for how we measure the performance of the people working inside it.

One of the most enduring challenges in our sector, communications, is how we measure, and more importantly demonstrate, success. The sector isn't unique in this regard. Lots of sectors have attribution challenges. But since the digital revolution, 'traditional communications' firms have found themselves competing for budgets against firms offering services that are significantly more measurable. For example, digital marketing and especially paid search engine marketing, which relies heavily on direct attribution, put our sector to shame when it comes to demonstrating success. With apologies to professionals in that sector who might balk at the deliberately round and low figures, conversations about return on investment can theoretically be as straightforward as: 'We spent your £500 budget on Google adverts for the search term "luxury men's shoes" and you acquired five new customers who spent £2,000 each in your online luxury shoe shop. Your £500 ad spend therefore generated £10,000 in revenue and you have a return on investment of 1,900 per cent. Would you like to run another campaign?'

Public relations is a lot more opaque than this. The sector has its own metrics, such as share of voice (SOV), which is a relatively sophisticated measure of how popular a brand is compared to its competitors, and equivalent ad value (EAV), which is a relatively crude metric that compares the cost of 'earned' media exposure (news stories, television appearances and so on) with their 'bought' equivalents (news adverts, product placements and so on). But businesses in the sector consistently struggle to demonstrate a direct link between the work they do and the client's bottom line.

For example, a PR campaign might see a client's spokesperson appearing on television, but it's impossible for us to robustly attribute all increases in website visits, product purchases or enquiries solely to that one event. We'd be able to point to any direct spike in website visits directly after the TV appearance as evidence of success, but what about the people who saw the TV interview and Googled the spokesperson the following week? Or people who watched the interview on repeat? Or saw it on Twitter months later? We can't necessarily claim any of those as one of our own victories. There's some correlation, and that's good, but we can't demonstrate causation in the same way. The client can very well argue that the increased website traffic the following week was due to something they did and we wouldn't be able to or necessarily want to dispute that.

Our solution to this problem is to deal solely in deliverables and not key performance indicators or return on investment. Rather than worrying about how our work impacts the client's bottom line, we agree with them in advance what we can feasibly deliver, and it's up to them to decide whether it's worth the money. That approach causes problems in and of itself because of our perceived reluctance to commit to events that are out of control. Some potential clients want us to explain how much more revenue they can expect to generate after investing in a PR campaign, and we can't do that and we don't want to. We'd be liars if we gave them a figure to hang their hats on. There's too much that we can't control. We can generate high levels of interest in a company among their target market and improve their reputation with consumers at the same time, but we can't control whether people buy from them. We could drive thousands of new visitors to their website but if their website crashes, there's nothing we can do. It's a challenge we face because our work straddles traditional media (hard to measure) and digital media (easier to measure).

The same challenges exist with the user experience work we do, but to a lesser extent. We can improve the wording on an online mortgage application while keeping it compliant with regulations, and then run user tests that clearly demonstrate a preference and higher conversion rate for our version compared to the old version, but we can't control interest rates or consumer confidence. So we could have the best application form in the world but have no impact on the bottom line. These are extreme examples to prove a point; we only worry about what we can control.

So while this approach does put us at a disadvantage when competing against companies that are able to accurately predict ROI, it gives us a big advantage in another way. We can map the deliverables we agree to with clients directly onto workflow within the business.

Getting the best out of remote workers with specific deliverables

Freelancers typically bill in one of three ways; they charge a day rate, they track their time, or they quote a price for a specific piece of work. We favour a slightly adapted version of the third approach. The first two approaches work well in lots of contexts but have certain disadvantages. Day rates work well for office scenarios because you simply turn up for your agreed number of days, do the work, then send the invoice. This model works great in a lot of scenarios and we've used it a few times, including paying for voice-over work in a recording studio and hiring some to moderate a usability test in a lab. Time tracking is OK for scenarios where the output has a strong link to the time spent doing it. In our industry, there are only a few tasks that match this description, for example some elements of analysis and reporting can be billed in this method.

Getting the best out of remote workers who track time

As mentioned, we do have some workers who bill us based on the hours they've put into a task rather than the number of completed units of work they've produced. These tasks are typically administrative, analytical, or research based and lend themselves fairly well to time-tracking because there's something approaching a linear relationship between input and output. One of the people who bills us in this way provides administrative and research support, and she is exceptionally good value for money. Not because she's cheap, but because she enjoys repetitive, analytical tasks and remains focused on them for extended periods of time.

She's rare in that regard and is able to complete in-depth reports far quicker and to a far higher standard than I ever could. She probably has a far greater impact on the smooth running of the business than she would give herself credit for. To make sure that she can work as effectively as possible and project her own revenues, while allowing us to manage our cash flow carefully, we want her to know what her minimum earnings from Essential Content will be. So, twice a year, we agree a minimum and maximum number of hours per month for the forthcoming six months. She then tracks her time using a browser add-on called Toggl, and sends us a report at the end of the month.

She completes a number of repetitive tasks each month, including invoicing and reporting, and as the number of clients in our business grows, the number of hours she needs to work grows with it. So there have been a few times where we've had to agree in the middle of a six-month period to increase the maximum number of hours she can put in.

Fostering autonomy

It's essential that remoteness serves the business and not the other way around. There's an acceptance across the business that everyone needs a degree of autonomy greater than what they might experience working in an office, where asking a senior colleague or manager for permission to take action on something can be done relatively quickly. We don't want permissions – or more specifically the time wasted waiting for them – to become a bottleneck in our business processes, so we work to give each person the absolute maximum range of permissions required in order to work as effectively as possible.

This approach can only work with the understanding and consent of clients. We've found over time that what started out as a necessity for us to function efficiently as a remote business has actually delivered a number of benefits for our clients. Here's one example. In our public relations work, we're regularly required to draft quotes on behalf of client spokespeople. These types of quotes generally come in two types: proactive and reactive. Proactive quotes are fairly straightforward; the client wants to say something about what's happening with their business, research it has conducted, or about something predictable, such as the increase in demand for packaging around Christmas. We draft the quote and the client approves it ahead of time. Reactive quotes are a little trickier because there's a significantly shorter notice period for approval. What normally happens in these scenarios is that a piece of news will break and the media will solicit insights and opinions from experts. If we represent such an expert, we are then in a race against other agencies representing our competitors to get our quotes written, approved and distributed. Quite often, the approvals process can really slow us down in taking advantage of these opportunities. It's especially disadvantageous when we account for the fact that we're competing for media coverage against brands with in-house communications teams. In-house teams are designed to be quicker off the mark, often with fewer hurdles to clear before they can get something approved and distributed.

Our way of mitigating this challenge is based on embracing the remoteness between members of our teams and between our teams and our clients. We do it in two ways. First, we invest a lot of time in predicting and anticipating the sorts of things our clients might be invited to comment on in the media. We prepare a calendar and write up a lot of different soundbites, talking points and insights that are essentially 'oven ready'. These are approved way in advance of us ever needing them. By having a bank of pre-approved material, we can often respond to media requests without bothering our clients at all. But not always. So we have to ask our clients to put their trust in us and let us speak on their behalf. We set some parameters around this. For example, we always get approval where possible and we don't speak on their behalf in all scenarios; sometimes we'd rather let an opportunity go than speak on behalf of our client without their prior approval if we think doing so presents too high a risk. But in some scenarios, when an opportunity feels too good to miss, and with our clients' written permission to do it, we are able to craft quotes attributable to them to help us react quickly. Not all of our clients sign up for this and we are fine with that. The clients that do agree to this are typically happy to do it because it saves them from being disturbed when they are particularly busy. This is especially useful for clients in different time zones. But it only works because we've been able to demonstrate our competence and understanding of their communications goals, their opinions and their attitude to risk.

People who work with us appreciate the high levels of autonomy our way of working affords them, although it does take some getting used to. It's a happy consequence of embracing remoteness and perhaps if we were an office-first type of business we wouldn't have had cause to contemplate just how much autonomy is useful and healthy. We understand that too much autonomy, where there are no observable boundaries or frameworks in place, will have the opposite effect to the one we're aiming for. So we always monitor the permissions we enact and reflect on what benefits and risks they bring.

No unscheduled calls

This is one of the harder-to-stick-to rules, and also the one that causes the most push-back when we explain it. It's also the rule that has had the biggest positive impact on the effectiveness of our communication as a group. There are plenty of good reasons for us to have this rule, but even if only for the fact that it completely removes periods of distracting, unstructured chat from our day it is worth keeping. Unscheduled phone calls are distracting, stressful and have an unacceptably low problem-solving success rate.

Why no unscheduled calls? First and foremost, calls are an interruption to workflow. They are in no way an adequate replacement for the unstructured and informal chats that are possible in an office environment. You simply cannot recreate that dynamic in a remote environment, so why waste the effort trying? When I pick up the phone to a colleague who is working remotely, I have no way of knowing how deeply engrossed they are in a piece of work. If they answer the phone, they have to immediately enter a totally new headspace. The amount of productivity or 'flow' that can be lost by this kind of interruption is not proportionate to the amount of time spent on the call. To enter a state of deep productivity and focus takes time, you can't just snap out of it and back into it. So calling someone without an appointment risks robbing them of that hard-earned deep focus for a minimum of the duration of the call, but more probably the length of the call plus at least 30 minutes to an hour to re-enter the state of concentration they were in before the call. Before we implemented this rule, the majority of out-of-the-blue phone calls made ended with some variation of 'I don't know, I'll find out and get back to you'. The follow-up would almost always come via email. In an office, it's easier to judge whether someone is open to being interrupted.

Unscheduled calls, in our opinion, are mostly an ineffective means of gathering or sharing information. There's a certain power dynamic at play which operates regardless of whom, if anyone, is most senior. When you make a call, you (hopefully, but not always) have an idea of what you want to talk about, what outcomes you expect and an understanding of how intense, demanding or uncomfortable the conversation is going to be. The recipient has none of this knowledge upfront. The recipient, even if they are not in a state of deep engagement with their work, may not be primed to answer any of the questions, which means the call is ultimately pointless because there is no guarantee of a quality response.

There are other reasons for not having unscheduled calls too. They display a lack of respect for the recipient's time and, to a lesser extent, their privacy. Because we don't require people working with us to keep fixed hours, we have no idea whether they're in work mode or not. For all we know they could be sleeping or out with family. But we do understand that most people's instinct when they see a co-worker's number come on their phone is to assume it's important and answer it.

We strongly encourage people to schedule calls, because it introduces a necessary element of friction into the process of communication. It's very easy just to pick up the phone to someone else and feel like you've moved the needle on solving a problem. To schedule the call, the person has to consider quite carefully what they want to get out of it, what they want to discuss, how long the call will last and what information will be required to make the call useful. They need to put this in writing to schedule the call, and nine times out of ten by the time they've done that they've most likely composed an email that is entirely suitable for getting what they need. We encourage people to think 'Could this call be an email?' If not, then fair enough, by all means set up a call.

How to schedule calls

The following is going to make Essential Content sound like a boring, rules-obsessed place to work. Hopefully that's not true but if I were reading our policy on scheduling a call I'd probably think it was. The purpose of having rules around call scheduling isn't to constrain freedom of communication but to support it.

1 Notice is important. We discourage people from scheduling same-day calls. If our other working practices are being observed, most people will have their day planned out already, so even if the call is proposed for three or four hours in the future, it will serve as an interruption.

2 We encourage people to schedule calls roughly near the beginning or the end of the working day and certainly not in the middle. This is based on my own experience of how I typically behave when there's a call in the diary. I daren't start any meaningful work during the hour before the call is scheduled because I know that at most I will have less than 60 minutes of uninterrupted focus. The chances are I'll hit my stride just as my calendar alert pings. So I'm reluctant to use that time for anything particularly useful, so in many cases it becomes lost time.

3 Call requests have to be accompanied by a brief agenda, outlining the context, purpose and anticipated outcome of the call. For example, if the person requesting the call expects the other person

to take a specific action after the call, it's helpful to communicate that in advance. If they want information, the agenda should include specific requests for any data or other information that is unlikely to be sitting at the front of a person's mind. There's nothing worse than being caught out on a call by someone asking for data. Even if knowing that data is part of a person's job, we can't realistically expect them to be able to recall anything and everything on the fly, so if you need data or specific information from a call and you want it to be accurate and up-to-date, give the other person the chance to find it and prepare it for your consumption.

4 Set a hard time limit. This is really important. Calls naturally drag on when there is no specified cut-off point. People are naturally reluctant to enforce their own boundaries when on a call because they worry about seeming rude. Both Zoom and Bluejeans are useful platforms to use in this regard because they have in-built features that allow you to limit the length of a call. They both give users a warning that they're running out of time. I'd much rather people scheduled a follow-up call than ran over their pre-arranged time slot because nobody was prepared to say 'I need to go.'

5 Decide on a platform and preferably share the link in advance. We use lots of different communication platforms, including Slack, Google Meet, Skype, FaceTime, WhatsApp, Bluejeans and Zoom. It can be immensely frustrating waiting for the person calling you to let you know how they're going to get in touch. A lot of these platforms take a little while to load so it saves time and frustration if the recipient of the call is able to get set up in advance. The most important reason for specifying the platform you want to use is that it lets the other person know whether they're going to be on video or not and allows them to make the necessary arrangements, such as setting up their headset, putting the cat in another room, tidying up behind them, sorting out their hair, moving the computer to somewhere that affords them more privacy, has better lighting and so on.

Exceptions to this rule include:

- Onboarding new starters: People new to the business are more than welcome to request short notice calls if they need. We have a scheduled meeting after three months and discuss whether the new starter still feels they need this option. In most cases it's not necessary after the onboarding period.

- Designated collaborative periods: We set aside periods of time for collaborative creative work. During these periods, it's necessary and useful to run things past one another. I personally think the relative 'novelty' of having unstructured back-and-forth compared to our usual way of working enhances the creative process.

- Emergencies that require immediate attention that otherwise risk the financial health of the business or its clients: There have only been a few unscheduled 'emergency' calls made since we introduced this policy. If a client's website has been hacked for example, everyone working in the businesses knows we need to break our rule to fix the problem.

- Opportunities that require immediate attention that would otherwise mean one of our clients misses out: Sometimes when working in public relations, opportunities pop up that need an almost immediate response. For example, if a broadcaster wants to set up an interview with a client. We have processes in place that enable us to respond to these requests without making unscheduled phone calls, but they rely on people being contactable during specific times. If the opportunity arises outside of these hours, we can and do resort to unscheduled calls.

'Brief me like I'm five'

Historically, the biggest point of friction with remote work as it relates to running Essential Content has been with the briefing process. We employ a lot of very experienced writers and subject matter experts of different types, and strive to always match the writer with the tasks that best suit their experience, ability and interests. But because we don't have the option to sit next to each other and point at our screens, and because screen sharing isn't always a suitable alternative due to time zone differences and sometimes language barriers, our standard approach is to always brief projects in writing, using a templated briefing document.

We've lost time and money more times than I'd care to remember due to someone misinterpreting or misunderstanding the brief. The former is usually worse because when someone thinks they've got the brief right but haven't, they'll go ahead and complete the work and then have to redo it or fix it. At least when they don't understand it they flag it up and ask for clarifications before investing their time and our budget into it. When this used to happen, it was treated entirely as the fault of the person providing the brief (normally myself). Even in cases where we thought we'd been sufficiently clear in a brief, there is literally no incentive for someone to get it wrong on purpose, so we adopted a policy of always blaming the messenger.

Having looked back over a handful of cases where our briefing process fell down, we identified that the problem was always linked to the absence of the personal contact, nuance and back-and-forth that would exist in a face-to-face briefing. It's incredibly easy to make assumptions about what the person reading the brief knows, understands and infers, and the things they don't. Things that would easily have been ironed out in the natural flow of a face-to-face conversation were being left open to interpretation. So our only two choices were to find a way to brief work in a way that would never, or only very rarely, require further clarification, or abandon remote work entirely. The most common misinterpretations were around the following things:

- Terminology – Essential Content has a number of clients in regulated sectors such as finance and insurance. These sectors are absolute hotbeds of (sometimes needlessly) complex lingo that often varies by geography.

- Compliance requirements – If something looks clumsily worded or overly verbose, the chances are it's got to be that way for regulatory reasons. Nevertheless when you're paying someone to improve a company's communication and don't highlight which bits they can't mess with, you're asking for problems.

- Format – This is the area where assuming knowledge was our downfall. It's very easy to get used to how a client likes their work delivered and assume that new writers have picked up on that by reviewing previous work. It's far easier to spell it out or use a restrictive template that doesn't allow for deviation.

- Word count – Yes, something as simple as word counts can be an expensive source of confusion. We had a policy early on of allowing writers to produce as much copy as they felt necessary in order to fulfil a brief, assuming that the depth of the topic at hand would provide a natural constraint. This proved embarrassingly wrong a few times before we started applying maximum word counts. Otherwise, writers would always write more content than we could use.

The solution to the problem came in the form of a joke from a financial services copywriter who'd been struggling to get his head around a particular brief. We'd arranged a call and, as we were working through the problem, I felt the need to apologise for patronizing the writer, someone with far more experience than myself and more knowledge of the subject matter, for what I thought was a classic example of 'telling someone how to do their job'. The response contained the solution. 'No, please explain it to me like I'm five.'

It was part joke – there's a popular 'subreddit' on the internet forum Reddit called 'explain like I'm five' in which lay people solicit experts to help them get their heads around all manner of things from animal nutrition to quantum mechanics – and part plea to dispense with needless deference and focus on clarity of message. So we took it and ran with it. Every new freelancer we recruit gets an apology in advance for the potentially patronizing style of our briefs.

We have six rules for writing our briefs:

- Provide an overview.
- Start every paragraph with a verb.

- Never use acronyms without explaining them.
- Explain the client's objective.
- Explain the risk of doing nothing.
- Link to every resource you mention.

Embracing remoteness

I don't like offices. I dislike them for a number of legitimate reasons: they're germ factories, they're always too hot or too cold, and they often contain people I would cross the street to avoid. I also dislike offices for entirely unreasonable reasons that I struggle to justify other than just by sticking with 'I don't care, I don't like them.' Without necessarily realizing it, my petty refusal to make my peace with the traditional workplace has informed not only where and how I work, but the entire culture and structure of Essential Content, the clients we have, the work we deliver and the people we recruit.

Every policy, strategy and process within the business is designed to work in concert with a distributed workforce. There is no friction between remoteness and 'how we used to do things' because we've always been remote.

It will be tempting for a lot of businesses adapting now to remote work to try to transplant as much of their office-based procedures, processes, culture and expectations onto an entirely different model. Essential Content didn't suffer from this issue because the objective was to create an environment that bore as few similarities as possible to an office setting. We never saw remoteness as a compromise, and because what we were doing was a relative novelty at the time, we were spurred on to go against the grain of traditional work practices, habits and orthodoxies, rather than trying to incorporate those into a framework that would bend them out of shape.

Of course, nobody associated with the business, myself, the people I work with or our clients realized that what we were attempting to do might one day become the norm. We were quite happy with our approach being relatively unusual and finding ways to succeed because of the remoteness, not in spite of it.

08

Remote culture tools, hacks and techniques

If you're ever lucky enough to be staying at the five-star Balmoral Hotel in Edinburgh, head up to the fifth floor and walk along the corridor to room 552. The door to this room is not like the others. For starters, it's the only door in the hotel decorated with an ornate bronze owl. The owl was fitted to the door to commemorate the fact that is the room in which author J K Rowling managed to finish *Harry Potter and the Deathly Hallows*, the seventh and final book in the Harry Potter series. Rowling completed her manuscript on 11 January 2007, and the book was released for sale on 21 July the same year. It sold 11 million copies on its first day and became the world's fastest selling book.

Admittedly, writers' retreats are not a new thing. And Rowling's extended stay at a luxury hotel isn't something we can all go and do when we feel the need to knuckle down to something, but her approach is worth contemplating. Rowling typically did her writing work from home. She told Oprah Winfrey in an interview: 'As I was finishing *Deathly Hallows*, there came a day where the window cleaner came, the kids were at home, the dogs were barking, and I could not work, and this light bulb went on over my head and I thought, "I can throw money at this problem"' (Schaub, 2016).

Some jobs, historically at least, lend themselves pretty well to remote working. In fact, in some cases remote is the optimum format. Remoteness is the point. A master luthier would be unlikely to build their best guitars working from a workshop with 30 other people, each one also making guitars, occasionally stopping by to chat, asking for advice and scheduling meetings. The same goes for lots of other professions. Consider work that requires prolonged focus on a single task, such as software coding or – dare we say it – writing a book. When was the last time you heard someone say 'I've really got to concentrate, so I'm going into the office'?

Rowling's decision to 'throw money' at her problem is what author Cal Newport describes in his seminal book *Deep Work* (Newport, 2016) as 'the grand gesture'. He describes it almost like a hack, albeit an expensive one, to trick the mind into focusing better. 'By leveraging a radical change to your normal environment, coupled perhaps with a significant investment of effort or money, all dedicated toward supporting a deep work task, you increase the perceived importance of the task. This boost in importance reduces your mind's instinct to procrastinate and delivers an injection of motivation and energy' (Newport, 2016).

Newport's thinking revolves around the idea that there are two types of work: deep and shallow. Work done while distracted, shallow work, adds minimal value to the world and is easily replicated, essentially exposing the person doing it to the risk of being made jobless by automation. And we all do the kind of 'shallow work' Newport describes: updating spreadsheets, sifting through emails, planning tasks and roadmapping projects are some common examples. He sees these tasks as anathema to adding value to a business or organization. Those of us who spend more time on shallow work, according to Newport, are more vulnerable. He advocates an approach that optimizes for what he describes as 'professional activities performed in a state of distraction-free concentration that push your cognitive capabilities to their limit. These efforts create new value, improve your skill, and are hard to replicate.'

Newport also cites psychoanalyst Carl Jung as an example of achieving extraordinary professional accomplishments by arranging one's life to allow for deep working. In the 1920s, Jung was in the process of challenging some of the theories developed by his friend and former mentor Sigmund Freud. As Newport describes, this was certainly a 'bold' move and Jung knew he needed to be on his A-game. So he extended the Swiss cottage he'd recently bought, adding a tower, to which he retreated for a minimum of two uninterrupted hours per day, for hyper-focused bursts of work. The work he did in his secluded tower formed the basis of what we now know as analytical psychology. He went on his extended retreats to rural Switzerland 'not to escape his professional life', as Newport explains, 'but to advance it' (Newport, 2016).

Obviously, Jung's professional feats were rare and unusual. And they weren't solely down to his choice to take leave from his daily clinical work to create space in his mind for thinking big thoughts. He *was* Carl Jung after all. But Newport's argument isn't about achieving world-changing schools of thought that influence generations, it's about operating at the peak of your intellectual capacity for as long as possible. Newport believes that the process of straining your intellect in these periods of uninterrupted and enjoyable focus actually increases it.

Ross, the energy auditor we heard from earlier, had an unexpected opportunity for deep work during the first Covid-19 lockdown. 'I tend to be more productive in the mornings and less in the afternoons, so it balances out overall,' he explains.

Ross didn't really perceive his own job as having much capacity for deep work. 'In the early days of working from home, when full lock downs were in place, I wasn't particularly productive, but this is because most of my contractors were also in lockdown, so I spent a couple of months logging in, doing some basic admin and keeping things ticking over.'

This reaction is entirely understandable. We often need to feel like we're doing something when there's simply not much to do. And without many available options for 'signalling' our value by creating outputs, these moments of low intensity can actually become quite stressful. Such scenarios can often give us an interesting choice to make. Some people will happily 'phone it in' until the work picks up, assuming that the peaks and dips of cognitive demand balance out eventually. Other people, and Ross is apparently one of them, see a lull in their regular workflow as an opportunity to go deep on something else. 'I did take the opportunity to learn how to do a few new things, things like learning how to pay contractors properly, which had been done previously by our admin team, but I can't say that every day was a school day,' he explains.

'However, with the lockdown in place I was able to focus on a couple of projects that I had been putting off due to not having any time, so I was able to bring in our first solar PV measures installed in support of the Energy Company Obligation. The company had been trying to find some way of bringing in solar PV for years, so finally being able to sit down and crack that problem is one of my big achievements since I started working here.'

Remote working is an opportunity for certain types of workers to pull themselves into focus, to resist the lure of distraction, to get behind themselves and push. Ross perceived his remoteness and the disruption to his regular workflow as an opportunity to gain greater focus and go deep. That he now considers the outcome of that perception as his biggest achievement since starting with his current employer highlights just how rewarding, for both employer and employee, it can be to foster or even 'curate' opportunities for depth.

Working remotely for these people is more than merely getting rid of the travel season ticket and having a lie in. It could completely revolutionize their approach to work. And it's important to remember that remote doesn't have to mean 'from home'.

Peter Shankman is the founder of Help A Reporter Out (HARO). It's an email-based service that connects reporters with sources, or the PR representatives of those sources. Shankman, who has attention deficit hyperactivity disorder (ADHD), revealed in a 2016 blog post that he'd found a novel solution to avoiding distraction and focusing on a deep work task. He booked a return flight from Newark, New Jersey to Shanghai, China. He had no intention of visiting Shanghai on this trip. He didn't even leave the airport. Shankman's entire trip was designed to keep him in the sky for approximately 30 hours there and back, free from distractions. In those 30 hours, Shankman claims he wrote 28,482 words (Shankman, 2016) of his book *Faster Than Normal*. Shankman's approach literally took off and garnered a lot of attention. His key message from the resultant media attention was to encourage people looking to achieve focus and results to carve out time to focus on one thing.

Many organizations already embrace the concept of the grand gesture, perhaps without realizing it. Corporate away-days are among the most common. So some are partially bought-in already, they just need to find ways to help people to recreate the same environmental dynamics while working away from the office. And in set-ups where most people work remotely, that could ironically mean getting everybody on-site. Or, it could mean something else entirely.

It's a little easier to approximate Shankman's 'focus on one thing' approach. And being remote gets us part of the way there already. Offices are full of distractions. It'd be a huge waste of an opportunity if organizations simply asked their workers to recreate the company office at home, pinging notifications and screen clutter included. Shankman advocates a clutter-free ethos for screen and desk, recommending OmmWriter as a distraction-free alternative to Microsoft Office, Apple's Pages or Google Docs for people working on documents, 'OmmWriter is essentially a blank canvas for your writing. Unlike Word or Pages, it doesn't have a lot of fancy menus or tools, it's simply a white page on a stunning snow scene background, that takes up your entire screen. It blocks out all system notifications as well, so all you have in front of you is your words' (Shankman, 2016).

Managers who embrace the informal principles of 'deep work', such as the grand gesture and laser focus on one task, stand to benefit enormously from what comes out of it. And almost every office-based job, regardless of its inherent seniority or expertise, has scope for going deep. Some jobs have more scope than others, for sure, but if you do it at a desk, there's at least part of your job that should theoretically allow you to shut out distractions and zone in on one singular task. Newport argues in *Deep Work* that this meaningful focus on a single task has benefits far beyond increasing productivity. He likens it to craftsmanship. 'Throughout most of human history, to be a blacksmith or a wheelwright wasn't glamorous. But this doesn't matter, as the specifics of the work are irrelevant.

The meaning uncovered by such efforts is due to the skill and appreciation inherent in craftsmanship – not the outcomes of their work' (Newport, 2016).

'I used to set aside admin days once a fortnight which are days that I know don't require customer calls or FaceTime,' explained Nathan, who works for Salesforce. 'I would explore local cafes and restaurants to work from for a morning or afternoon. As long as they had power and a reasonable internet connection, I was set. Walking to these venues helped focus the mind, and walking home helped switch off. Lockdown obviously chained me to my home office desk.'

His experience might be instructive for two different reasons. First, it demonstrates that some employers had already embraced a hybrid working model and their workers were benefiting from it. Second, it shows us that it's possible to go deep on a task even if that task itself isn't one of Cal Newport's 'value adding' tasks. Nathan had found a way to segment his time to suit the natural dynamics of his own energy and productivity. It's the kind of thing a worker can only really achieve when their employer gives them a degree of autonomy. It's ironic that the almost universal switch to remote working curtailed this for him. As employers adapt to fully remote or hybrid working models, they should be promoting this kind of approach to work.

Are established methodologies fit for purpose?

SEO specialist Zorica, who we heard from in Chapters 5 and 6, believes the existing processes and procedures her organization relied on required just a little tweaking to make them work well remotely. 'My role requires a lot of focus so I've found that for certain tasks I'm more productive at home. That also applies to some things that require collaboration with other people, such as hopping on a quick Zoom call, which in my experience can solve most things.' Although she does notice an increase in resistance when trying to achieve a more collaborative dynamic from home.

She's found mainstream, non-specialist collaborative tools including Zoom, Slack, Google Drive, Google Docs, Google Sheets and Google Calendar have been more than good enough to facilitate collaboration in most contexts. It's almost her entire collaborative ecosystem. But there are limitations.

'For things like side-by-side with other team members, starting a new project from scratch or holding an ideation session, I've found that in-person interaction is really more useful and productive. We can fix roadblocks faster, things go smoother and you can address and answer certain questions while everyone is there so you avoid repetitions.

'I usually set the two or three most important tasks I want to complete for the day, and I just focus on that. I also batch similar tasks together so my attention is not all over the place. Although it's not always possible, I try to have a dedicated day for meetings so I squeeze them all in. Or if I'm proofreading or optimizing articles then I just focus on that.

'Where I am, we work in autonomous teams. It means that it's up to us to decide what we will prioritize and which problem we'll focus on solving next. It's all about agility. And in our SEO team things are pretty flexible – we don't track time and everyone has freedom to organize their working day. All that matters is that we move towards completing our key performance indicators.'

It's already becoming clear that we need to at least tweak the working practices that have served us well in the context of the office. In some cases, organizations will need to ask themselves some honest questions about whether the formal practices they've relied on are fit for purpose in a future that will unavoidably involve hybrid ways of working. Rachel, who works for the Scottish government, has a complex role. She's observed a number of challenges that are likely to be common among big, complex organizations. She's optimistic about the potential for remote working, but thinks some of the techniques being lauded the most have so far failed to live up to their potential as a source of liberation and improved efficiency.

'I work in a service design delivery team. That means we're designing a new government service, working with designers, policy colleagues, developers, analysts and product owners. From my perspective, one of the big challenges we have with remote working is organizing all of these different workstreams. This is something software developers know too well, and that's why they typically use Agile delivery methods. It helps them track tasks through the development cycle and monitor progress.'

For context, Agile is a set of principles informing management and workflow methodology born out of software development. It is based on an idea of iterative development and differs from other established methodologies in a few important ways. First and foremost, Agile is characterized by the idea of continual improvement, adaptive planning and self-organizing teams. It demands that practitioners are not wedded to a specific set of requirements and welcomes changing requirements, even late in development. Agile processes harness change for the customer's competitive advantage (Beck et al, nd). One of the key components of the Agile methodology is the 'sprint'. A sprint is essentially a time box with a predefined end point during which teams aim to complete as much of the work as possible. The theory is that sprints help teams break down large and complex projects into manageable chunks of work. Theoretically, at the end of each sprint, the 'product' will have improved. Every sprint features four Agile 'ceremonies': planning; stand-up (essentially a brief daily meeting focused on identifying blockers to progress); review; and retrospective, in that order.

What is now a global movement adopted by major organizations around the world started life as a simple 24-word manifesto:

> Individuals and interactions over processes and tools
> Working software over comprehensive documentation
> Customer collaboration over contract negotiation
> Responding to change over following a plan.
>
> (Beck et al, nd)

On paper, Agile seems like the ideal framework to support remote work, especially the elements that focus on self-organization and cross-functional teams. But to the people actually doing the work, like Rachel, it's not as simple as that.

'I keep seeing Agile delivery being used to monitor product and service development. The trouble is, we don't work in this way: tasks like user research and iterating content take time and can't always be completed in one sprint. So, instead, Agile delivery is used as a way to monitor our productivity and make sure we're constantly delivering.

'I have real concerns about this way of working. It basically means that you're "on" for weeks and months on end (I'm on month five). During lockdown, I've noticed managers and senior leaders being overly preoccupied with Agile ceremonies – because they can't "see" whether we're busy. So I spend a lot of my time talking in stand-ups, saying how busy I am, and taking part in "show and tells" and "retros". These activities are also about showing how productive we are. It's particularly frustrating because Agile ways of working weren't intended as a measure for being busy. In the design context, it should be about learning quickly and iterating services. Instead, we're focused on the following things: How big is this task? How long will it take to finish? How many hours do you have in a day? When will you finish it and move on to the next thing?

'On top of all of this, of course, is the performative aspect of it. I've already mentioned daily stand-ups (which take up about three hours of my working week) and then having to showcase my "outcomes" at show and tells. In some ways, it's quite dehumanizing. Like my only real value is how quickly I can get something done. I feel it all boils down to a lack of trust. Managers not being sure if we're delivering as efficiently as possible. Senior leaders being unsure they're getting value for money. Policy colleagues being sceptical of the user-centred design process and needing regular updates to show we're doing the best work we possibly can.

'In the long term, I worry about burn out. There's such emotional labour attached to this way of working. It feels like service design is a type of theatre: where we're all trying to prove ourselves in an increasingly competitive market, whilst also still needing to prove ourselves to the people who hired us in the first place. Perhaps it's a sign of design immaturity in a large, old-fashioned organization. For me, this is only partly true. Fundamentally we still don't trust people to work in a way they see fit.'

09

Rules and etiquette

Workplaces have always fostered a degree of acceptable inequality, often accidental but sometimes by design. We're not talking about pay inequality or deliberate discrimination here. The types of 'acceptable inequalities' that we see in organizations are typically anchored in concepts of seniority. The CEO might have their own parking space, for example. The idea of the desirable corner office as a metaphor for status and prestige is predicated on inequality; corner offices are only desirable because not everyone gets to sit in one. If everyone worked in a cubicle of identical dimensions, there'd be less inequality, but everyone would be working in a cubicle, which is not a standard to which any organization should aspire.

Be mindful of avoidable inequalities

One of the benefits of a centralized office is that organizations can do a lot to remove unnecessary inequalities and foster a drive toward equity. The CEO might still have her own parking space, but an employee with mobility limitations may get one too. In an office, everyone typically sits on the same kind of chair, at the same kind of desk, has access to the same kind of food, connects to the same WiFi and uses the same software. This uniformity is an organizing principle of what makes an office an office. They might be dreary 'interruption factories', but at least they're fairly equitable. With a distributed workforce potentially spread around the entire world, it's not always possible to control for these inequalities.

Assuming for a short moment that everyone not in the office is working from home, and not at a co-working space or in their local coffee shop, the potential for quite visible and significant inequalities becomes clear. The first, and perhaps most obvious, inequality is space. Not everyone has the same amount of it. Sean recalls a conversation from very early on in his career with a manager who was complaining about how he'd spent the majority of the weekend cutting his lawn, despite owning a sit-down lawnmower. 'I don't begrudge anyone for having a massive garden, and I was well aware that this colleague's salary was probably four times the size of mine, but having an unmanageably large garden wasn't a complaint I could sympathise with while living in a small, one-bedroom flat.'

Video-calling has given us a portal into the home lives of our colleagues. There's obviously potential for fun – pets and children often pop up, we get to see what books our workmates read (or want us to think they read) and what art they've got on their walls – and it offers a chance to get to know the people we work with on a new level. But it can also create friction where it didn't exist before. Think about appraisals. In an office, these normally get done in a meeting room. The manager and her direct report sit on the same sort of chair at the same desk, enjoying the same ambient temperature. Remote appraisals suffer from a lack of equity. A junior employee working from the kitchen in a shared house, possibly belonging to their parents, may have to grind their teeth through an appraisal with their manager who is sitting in their comfortable and spacious home office, at a large desk, on a comfortable chair, with enough room for all of the home-working accoutrements they want. In Spring 2021 UK home improvement chain Wickes launched a new TV advert as part of their 'house-barassment' campaign. The 30-second clip centred around a work video call and 'Claire', a woman so embarrassed by the tatty condition of her home that she refuses to switch off her novelty background when her boss asks her to. The advert was supposed to be a joke, but there's a grain of truth in there.

It's not the manager's fault she has more space at home than the people in her team. And organizations shouldn't seek to patronize their people by pretending that some people aren't significantly better paid than others and can afford to live in a larger house. They should, however, find ways to remove avoidable sources of inequality. Many organizations caught onto this quickly, sending out office furniture, monitors and providing support so their employees could approximate many of the workplace equalities they had in the office.

Lottery winner testimonials

Organizations should also seek, where possible, to avoid creating frameworks and policies for remote work that favour the sorts of employees who would naturally gravitate toward home working anyway. These might be senior team members who've passed through the phase of their career where networking with and observing more experienced people benefits them. They may also be people who are necessarily more effective when working alone on an engaging task rather than cooperating and collaborating with a range of other stakeholders. A contributor to the Works In Progress blog using the pseudonym John Uskglass coined the phrase 'lottery-winner testimonial' to describe the dangers of biasing to the experience of outliers. It very neatly summarizes a potential problem for managers dealing with remote staff. Some stand to gain so much more than others. To that end, methods of soliciting and processing feedback from workers should be designed to accommodate the 'lottery losers' as well as the winners. These 'lottery losers' might include some of the following: vulnerably housed people, people dealing with domestic issues, new starters, people returning to work after a period of absence such as sabbatical, paternity or illness, workers prone to presenteeism (we've all known a colleague who has literally had to be sent home rather than staying home), people in a phase of career transition who need training, people subject to performance reviews – the list goes on.

Remote communication habits

Of the list of potential lottery losers above, new starters arguably pose the largest challenge to organizations seeking to smooth out the wrinkles in their own remote work policies. The unique circumstances of the pandemic in which many people started a new job, or even entered the workforce for the first time, has highlighted weakness in various parts of corporate life. Not least in how we communicate.

'In some ways video calls are even better than face-to-face encounters in the office,' said Manchester-based marketing executive Nicole Rouwenhorst. She enjoyed starting her new job during lockdown and believes that the less formal environment in which she first encountered her colleagues softened the edges of what is traditionally a potentially formal, rigid experience. 'You'll find out, "Oh, they've just got an Asos package, I like Asos too." It just sparks conversations' (Shaw, 2020).

Henry Moffett's experience of meeting new colleagues wasn't quite so pleasant. The 34-year-old had moved jobs after spending seven years with his previous employer. 'It was surreal, waving gormlessly at 50 people from the sofa in my flat,' he recounts of his first introductory video call. 'When you can't fall back on the nuances [you pick up] in physical meetings, it can be difficult to judge how things are going,' he told the BBC in an interview (Shaw, 2020). 'Silences during traditional meetings aren't unusual, but on virtual meetings it feels like they need filling.'

Video calls are perhaps the defining feature of remote work. There's more to it than that, but without Zoom, Teams, Skype and the likes, we simply wouldn't have been able to retain anything close to a sufficient degree of 'in-person' interaction in order to approximate the natural rhythms of a working day. But video calling has discrete but important differences to in-person meetings, and the longer we use these platforms, the more troublesome they can become.

As Henry points out, there's also the issue of having to look at your own face for extended periods of time. 'It's surprisingly draining because you are so hyper-aware of how you are presenting yourself' (Shaw, 2020).

The obvious solution to this particular part of what's been dubbed 'Zoom fatigue' is to turn off the camera and treat the meeting as an audio call. But of course it's not that simple. Turning off the camera when others have kept theirs on disrupts the equilibrium. And it creates anxiety. Workers wonder how they'll be judged for 'going dark'. Will their colleagues think they're not fully engaged in the call? Are they doing something else? What are they trying to hide.

Lydia Mack, a Los Angeles-based copywriter, told CNN for a feature entitled 'Stop making employees turn on webcams during meetings': 'If it's a team meeting and I'm the only one with my camera off for an extended period of time, it can also be a distraction [for others] and leave them wondering if I'm even at my computer, heard the conversation in its entirety, and so on' (Murphy Kelly, 2021). And in any case, some employers simply won't let their workers go dark, even if they are tired of looking at their own face.

'I was on a call with about 15 employees and [the speaker] said everyone should have their camera on because it's company policy and part of our culture now,' said a New York City-based non-profit employee to CNN for the same feature, who'd declined to be named in the interview for fear of company retaliation. The employee told her employer that being on camera caused her anxiety (Murphy Kelly, 2021).

It's hard not to become furious with her employer on her behalf. And her experience is a very stark example of how organizations can lazily throw around notions of 'culture' to justify harmful decisions. 'I told them being on camera causes me anxiety and didn't turn it on. I eventually got a doctor's note' (Murphy Kelly, 2021).

Rachel, who we heard from in the last chapter, believes the trade-offs of remote work threaten to undermine the benefits. 'I joined a new team during lockdown and have experienced both ends of the remote work spectrum: feeling like I had more control over my day-to-day interactions, while also realizing I was in a constant battle.

'There are little things I really enjoy. I like being able to join remote meetings and deciding if I want to be seen or not. Being a woman, I've felt so conditioned to smile and be nice during my interactions with others that it's so liberating to join calls and frown, grumble, and roll my eyes without being called out for it. I can also sit with my dog on my lap, too, and he helps with stress.

'However, I'm quite aware that my boundaries are always being tested. A lot of older people don't like not being able to see you whilst having a conversation, and their needs are often prioritized, although I'm not quite sure why. Equally, when I've tried to do working hours better suited to my lifestyle (7.30–3.30), this was almost impossible when I moved into a service design and delivery team. If someone more senior wanted a meeting at 4pm, then I had to be there. So it wasn't worth my time to start early.

'Weirdly enough, I think this might be easier for parents. People generally understand if you've got kids and need to work within their time schedule. But being childless and without caring responsibilities, my needs feel pretty low in pecking order.'

Rachel's concerns about her boundaries and the trade-offs of remote working are well founded. Having to manage distributed workforces has caused some employers to become very touchy and overly assertive when it comes to respecting boundaries. There's a risk that managers and company owners will permit themselves to take liberties with their workers' wellbeing and privacy because they feel a sense of entitlement, having 'allowed' them to work from home. It's one of the problems we'll see arising from the toxic discourse from some quarters that characterizes those who prefer to work from home as 'lazy'. If enough people say it, there's a risk that employers will feel their employees owe them something in return for being able to work from home, government-mandated lockdowns notwithstanding. Employers should be wholly committed to mitigating the very real harms that can be caused by enforcing certain styles of communication, not wrapping them in notions of company culture to make them seem benevolent. These harms, as well as being bad in general for things like productivity and morale, perpetuate inequalities.

'Women tend to have higher self-presentation costs than men and are likely to feel heightened pressure to demonstrate competence by appearing extra vigilant on camera,' explains Professor Alison Gabriel of the University of Arizona, the author of a study into the effects of video conferencing on worker wellbeing (Murphy Kelly, 2021). 'Additionally, as women took on disproportionate childcare demands compared to men during the pandemic, they are more likely to have kids in the background, which could unfortunately call into question their ability to be committed to their work and their ability to focus. We also tend to hold women to higher standards for physical appearance. Being on camera can exacerbate all of these things.'

Video conferencing has other ways of making us feel uncomfortable, too. The experience of one person we interviewed for this book who didn't want to provide their name or where they work, was – by their own admission – verging on paranoia. 'I absolutely hate it when people are typing during video calls. If I'm speaking and I see someone typing, I convince myself they're sending someone else a message about me. The reason I think this is true is because I've done it myself. It's so easy. You're all plugged into Zoom for a video call and you've got Slack open in another tab. Boredom, or irritation gets the better of you and you want to vent. It's so easy to hop over to Slack into a private channel or direct message and talk to a colleague. But from the perspective of the person talking, I now know how horrible it feels. Ever since I noticed two people typing while I was speaking, I've become hyper-sensitive to it.'

Remoteness from colleagues can absolutely make personal interactions brittle. But how do personal interactions and relationships fare when we import the awkwardness and hesitancy of remoteness into a face-to-face context? In September 2021 the *Guardian* published a fascinating series of interviews with people who had started a job during lockdown and had then returned to the office to be with colleagues they'd only ever known virtually. 'I'm a woman in a male-dominated industry – and the only woman on my team,' explained Helen, a 29-year-old software developer from London (Hill, 2021). 'When we were working remotely, I think the fact that I didn't fit in was masked by the sort of formality that was imposed by virtual meetings.' Having considered the fact that she didn't fit in with the company's physical culture after feeling that she did quite well within its remote culture, Helen, echoing the concerns from one of our interviewes who was concerned he was being talked about behind his virtual back, ventured a similar concern; 'perhaps all the lads have been having lots of fun in direct messages on Slack all this time and I wasn't aware of the party I wasn't invited to,' she wondered.

Another contributor to the same article explained that physical interactions with her junior colleagues became strained very quickly once they were in physical proximity. 'I've spent a year building relationships with my team over Zoom but now we've met, we don't really know how to act around each other. It's like visiting a new country and trying to learn about the culture, while being trapped in a hotel room and only seeing people out of the window' (Hill, 2021).

Perhaps the most concerning testimony shared in the article was that of a 55-year-old woman who had joined a company after a remote recruitment process and who began to suspect her face, or, to be more specific, her wrinkles didn't fit. 'I strongly suspect that they would not have hired me, had they met me in person during the interview process,' said Alexandra, who had been with her new employer for 15 months when she spoke to the *Guardian*. 'Now I understand the chemistry of the office, I am certain that I only got the job because the process was virtual and I look younger than I am,' she explained. 'My much younger colleagues treat me completely differently now they've met me in person: they sideline me, I have to listen to them slagging off anyone over the age of 40 and joking about the menopause.'

Alexandra's experience speaks to a risk that all employers considering a hybrid model should be aware of. There will be cliques and allegiances based on a worker's personal circumstances and willingness (or ability) to attend the office. The employees they onboarded remotely may have a hill to climb to achieve a sense of belonging in an organization that has entire physical history behind it that they are not part of. Although these people may have been in post for nearly two years at the time of writing, they are still new starters in many regards. Trivial things will trip them up and make them feel like outsiders.

Managers need to find ways of fostering communication habits that are fit for purpose in a distributed workforce. A comment that would land perfectly well if delivered in person might be received differently via email. Everyone should know that email is not a reliable vessel for even the most well-observed irony. This brittleness can manifest in other ways, too. Steph, an urbanism consultant, recalls an example from one of her superiors that changed her entire approach to how she communicated with colleagues. A senior co-worker had asked for Steph's opinion on some work a member of another team had done. Steph believed the work needed a good deal of improvement.

'I wanted to be tactful, so I responded to her email to say I hadn't got time to review it thoroughly that day, but that I'd take a look the following day and send over some initial thoughts. The truth was that the work wasn't up to scratch and I needed some time to formulate a response that was constructive and sensitive. It wouldn't have been useful for anyone if I'd shared my immediate, unfiltered reaction. Within literally a minute or two of me sending that email, the same co-worker sent me a meeting invite for that afternoon entitled "colleague feedback processes".'

This passive-aggressive appointment setting is as good an example we'll see of remoteness robbing colleagues of their ability to empathise in the moment. Had the original conversation happened in person, it would have been almost impossible for the senior colleague to have reacted to Steph's appeal for more time by demanding a meeting with one hour's notice. By sending the meeting, Steph's colleague was trying to formalize the context in which they were communicating. If she couldn't get the feedback she wanted from a 'conversation', she'd get it by installing the formal parameters of a meeting between two colleagues, one of whom was senior to the other.

'It felt almost provocative to me', said Steph. 'Ever since that happened I've been scared to tell people I'm too busy to do something at that moment. I feel like if I can't react to what they need I risk getting pulled into yet another meeting. And since I already hate meetings, I'm more inclined to simply become reactive to other people's needs rather than managing my workflow in a way that works for me.'

How we speak to our colleagues has always been an important part of workplace culture. When we speak to them is now becoming an area for concern too.

Remote meeting etiquette

Steph's colleague may not have intended to come across as passive-aggressive. We might give her the benefit of the doubt in that respect, but – as many remote workers are now discovering – there's an acceptable window for scheduling meetings.

According to a study conducted in March 2021, 'Zoom fatigue' is a genuine and persistent problem for workers. The main causes for concern, according to the Chartered Institute of Personnel and Development's People Management publication, are 'a combination of prolonged eye contact, constantly seeing yourself in real time, restricted mobility and the cognitive load of trying to compensate for the absence of non-verbal cues' (Brown, 2021).

One way in which the office naturally attenuates the length and intensity of meetings is that meeting room space is finite. Let your meeting drag on for long enough and it'll eventually be curtailed by a polite knock or impatient bang on the door from the person upon whom's room booking you are impinging. Zoom and similar plat-forms remove that natural 'hard stop' and if meetings are not properly managed, they take up too much time, cost too much energy and sap motivation in equal proportion to the amount of time by which they have overrun.

There are lots of video conferencing tools and they do different things well. Zoom is great for audio and visual quality, for example. Slack's video calling feature is handy because it's integrated with the rest of the platform, so you can easily 'hop on a call' (more about 'hopping on calls' in a moment) to discuss a matter that threatens to outgrow its space in the relevant discussion channel. Verizon's video platform Bluejeans boasts of 'one-touch join' and 'user centric meeting controls'. At first glance, it looks just like the others. In our opinion, Verizon have buried the headline; the best thing about Bluejeans is that the meeting room function approximates an actual meeting room. You have to book in advance and if you arrive early or stay late, there is a very good chance you will end up crashing someone else's meeting or having your own meeting crashed. While this raises obvious privacy concerns, it will prove to be a very effective control on meetings dragging on longer than they need to. Zoom has a time-out feature which theoretically ensures meetings can only go on for a set amount of time, but that is easily bypassed simply by starting another meeting.

Video conferencing is arguably too easy. It lacks the natural friction of an in-person meeting that requires people to leave their desk and find an available space. And that fact, combined with a general anxiety among workers of wanting to appear to be busy, has led to an extreme overuse of this sort of software. Video meetings are a source of fatigue and anxiety due to one or all of the following, easily-mitigated factors: notice given, length, intensity, frequency and format.

'Can you hop on a call?' are possibly the five most dreaded words for remote workers. Your colleague could be in the middle of a high-focus task and prepping for a call takes them completely out of them flow state. People with children to look after who plan their working day meticulously can do without unscheduled interruptions too. And for people who simply haven't budgeted the time for an ad-hoc call, the time cost represents a major disruption to their plan. Short notice calls just don't work for everyone.

10

A hybrid future

Balancing physical and virtual culture

'Sensory overload!' came the first message into our 'Back to work' WhatsApp group. Nathan, who works in London for Salesforce, a Fortune 500 cloud computing firm, was back in the office. As people had started preparing to filter 'back to work' in late September 2021, we'd asked for volunteers to let us know how their first day back in the office had gone. We were expecting end-of-day summaries of how it went, with details related to being around colleagues again and the nuances of getting back into the swing of working from an old desk. Nathan gave us more of a running commentary, and it was interesting to get his observations as they happened. He evidently found it quite over-stimulating.

'Lots of construction projects around our office had been completed while the city was relatively empty, so it felt like our office had been picked up and moved. Also, I can no longer walk around London with headphones, you need your wits about you! New cycle lanes, lanes for electric buses and taxis, then you have to dodge the electric scooters and not trip over the ones that have been left on the streets. London is one big kid's bedroom!'

Dave Surgey, who works in London in the financial services sector, had also experienced sensory overload. 'The first thing that struck me was the smells. I didn't really notice them before Covid. I guess you just accept it of London, but you notice everything now. The pollution is clear even on a Friday when the roads are empty.'

Smell is probably the most overlooked sense when it comes to planning workplaces. Businesses spend millions on visual aesthetics, on ergonomic furniture, on managing acoustics, and, of course, some businesses – especially those that want to keep their staff on-site for longer – allocate a lot of budget to the food. Every building has its own smell and it's something we just accept. Probably because you stop noticing it after a while. It's when you return after a period of absence that the smell of the office can become highly evocative. Anyone who's gone back to their old school as an adult will know what we mean. It's intense. And, although it may not sound like it's that important, organizations might want to pay attention to things like this, for two main reasons. The first and most obvious is that some people will be hyper-sensitive to matters of hygiene. Bad or even just strong smells probably won't breed much confidence in that regard. Second, smells – even when there hasn't just been a global pandemic – can be distracting. A 2019 study by London property maintenance firm Aspect found that 85 per cent of office workers said the physical environment was 'unpleasant'. Sixty-five per cent said they didn't like how their place of work smelled (Bizley, 2019).

Organizations that enjoy a successful transition from office-centric to hybrid will have embraced large-scale change before their workers get back. Those that fail will be the ones that simply re-opened the doors and expected their people to return and feel comfortable.

Remote work skillset

There will come a time in the near future where the absence of a remote skillset will be incredibly limiting to a person's knowledge economy career. Experience and talent will still be in high demand, but only if the worker possesses the technical and social skills to use those assets in a remote or hybrid context. Even now, as we in the white collar workforce get used to remote collaboration, our remoteness is having an impact on how we deploy our skills.

One mundane but instructive example of this is document sharing and collaboration. We've been able to do this for years and most organizations have systems and platforms set up for it. But now the dynamics of collaboration have changed. A conversation with a solicitor working on behalf of an insurance company explained to us how being remote from her colleagues had created a new set of workplace anxieties. 'My job involves reviewing documents to ensure they're compliant before customers and members of the public can read them, so I'm often adding comments and edits to shared files. I've noticed since the switch to remote that significantly more people have access to the files that I work on. It's made me approach my work differently. The feeling of working in front of an audience makes me self-conscious and I am convinced I make more mistakes. So I've started copying documents into new files, working on them in private, then copying my changes back into the original. It takes longer, but I can focus better this way.'

When pressed on why she thinks more people can see her work now compared to before the switch to remote, our solicitor isn't quite sure. 'I think it might be something the company has implemented to compensate for people not being physically together. They want to make sure all stakeholders have access to important documents. But all I see is a long row of icons showing how many people are logged into that document. I'm sure half of them haven't even read it.'

This is a great example of an ostensibly location-agnostic practice – shared documents theoretically work well in offices and remotely – requiring some extra thought now that the distribution of employees has changed. The organization mentioned above has taken what it may think is a pragmatic approach; more people are working outside of the office therefore more people now need access to more documents. It's not that simple. Deciding who has access to a document, just like deciding who gets copied in on an email, shouldn't ever be about 'covering all bases'. Over-sharing in this way can lead to a range of unintended negative consequences. For instance, if someone has been given access to a document, do we assume therefore that they've seen it, or read it?

The hybrid approach should enable many different types of organizations to thrive, provided they are able to segment time and activities effectively. The traditional office-based approach to work takes for granted that most people will be in the same place at the same time. This assumption lends itself to lazy planning; if most people are in the office most of the time, a manager can easily call a short-notice meeting or pull together an informal gathering. And this is fine. But there are better ways to harness resource. A segmented approach has a lot going for it. If employees know in advance that they have a set period in one location to participate in a collaborative activity before relocating elsewhere alone to go deep into their own solo work, or even just to get their admin out of the way, they have the scope to greatly optimize the time their employers use. People can come together usefully for activities like planning, workshops and onboarding new clients, and then distribute to where they want to be to get things done.

Segmenting work in this way may also help to solve a problem that appears to be growing in certain sectors. The problem is best summed by the findings of an August 2021 study by global communications and media network PHD, which found that the time spent by so-called creative economy professionals on non-creative work has increased by 57 per cent in the last 10 years (Sanchez, 2021). Around the world, more than 88 per cent of people working in marketing say they spend most of their time on administrative tasks like reporting, tracking campaign performance, competitor analysis and producing audience insights. The 1,721 marketers surveyed also said they spend more time planning and analysing investments than they did 10 years ago.

Analysing the findings from the study, Campaign magazine reporter Sabrina Sanchez identified a counterintuitive trend: task automation is not liberating knowledge workers from the grind of admin as intended. 'As AI and automation become more widespread,' Sanchez notes, 'marketers are spending less time executing campaigns'. Sanchez highlights that marketing campaign execution-focused work, such as workshops, creating content and media relations, is slipping down the list of things marketers actually spend their time doing. She notes that execution-based tasks 'dropped from the fourth to the fifth most regularly carried out task over the past year, as well as producing campaigns, which dropped from the third to the fourth most frequent task.' Mark Holden, Strategy and Planning Director at PHD, was upbeat about what the findings might suggest for his industry. He observed that AI has the potential to liberate people from rote tasks so they can focus on more creative endeavours, noting that 'AI will enable a junior creative to operate as if they are an executive creative director,' adding that it 'will produce a range of [assets], and the creative can decide which ones they want to work with' (Sanchez, 2021).

We can forgive Holden's optimism, but his own data suggests that tools designed to free people from high-effort, low-skill tasks like creating reports so they can focus more on being creative are currently acting as a constraint. And it sounds like an industry culture issue, rather than a workplace environment problem. For years, marketers – especially those in digital – have had their feet held to the fire by clients when it comes to justifying expenditure. Despite consistently representing one the biggest investments a business traditionally makes, marketing has always suffered from an undeserved reputation as being a 'luxury'. And to that end budget holders demand more.

Organizations embracing the remote approach will need to allocate more budget to travel and accommodation. This will typically represent a fraction of what they might save from not having the running costs of a centralized office. 'When we surveyed our employees on how they want to be set up in the long term as we emerge from lockdowns and restrictions, the majority wanted flexibility,' wrote Kate Diver, Head of People Risk, Workplace and Expansions at international payment platform Wise (formerly TransferWise) in a company blog post (Diver, 2021). 'Flexibility to ditch the commute, to be around their families, to spend time with their loved ones anywhere in the world whilst collaborating and contributing to our mission. And we thought, why not?'

Wise has locations in 21 countries, including an HQ in Shoreditch, London, and offices in: Hong Kong; Zug, Switzerland; Tallinn, Estonia; Tampa, Florida and New York City, United States; Tokyo, Japan; Sydney, Australia; São Paulo, Brazil; Riyadh, Saudi Arabia; Mumbai, India; and

Cherkasy, Ukraine. The company is firmly committed to a hybrid future. In January 2021 they announced their policy of giving staff 90 days per year to work from anywhere they wanted. Diver explained the thinking: 'by giving our employees clarity, they're able to make longer term decisions about how and where they set up home.

'Our people need to work remotely for loads of reasons: staying with family during the pandemic, wanting to combine work and travel (one of our requests came from someone applying to work in the Seychelles!) and to give them more time with their loved ones. Our goal is to make living globally easier for our customers, so it makes sense that we make living globally easier for the people building Wise, too.'

Aside from organizations that have embraced the 'remote first' approach, it's been obvious for some months since the first lockdown that the majority of organizations would adopt a hybrid model. The hybrid model assumes there are benefits to both remote and office-centric. The challenges are twofold. First, organizations will need to find a solution that optimizes the respective benefits of remote work and office-based work; for example it'll be a poor use of everyone's resources to bring people into the office so they can perform high-intensity solo work. The second challenge is to overcome the idea that a hybrid model necessarily means having the best of both worlds. 'I want to work from home because my home already provides the perfect working environment' said no 20-something ever. Younger workers are more likely to live in house-shares. Balancing the various benefits and drawbacks of remote working is going to prove exceptionally difficult when age and location differences come into play.

The rise of autonomy

We all had precious freedoms curtailed during lockdown. For one demographic, though, when it came to work, at least, the leash significantly loosened. Junior and mid-level knowledge economy workers were among those to experience an increase in workplace freedom and autonomy. Their bosses hadn't collectively decided to loosen the reins and resist the temptation to over-manage. It was the simple consequence of remoteness. For some employees, their autonomy increased simply because it was impossible for their bosses to manage them to the degree to which they'd become accustomed. And, to be fair to employers, some of them really embraced it. One of our favourite examples of this is the cycling charity in Manchester that introduced 'meet-free Mondays', giving their people an entire day free of meetings and – perhaps more importantly – free from the threat of meetings.

In the controversial and highly influential book *Bullshit Jobs: A theory* (2018), anthropologist David Graeber makes a lot of compelling but depressing arguments. Among his most memorable arguments are that most jobs wouldn't be missed if they went away (he cites public relations consultants, one of the authors of this book's job, as an example) and that while technological advances should see us working less as more things become automatable, we're actually finding new and pointless ways to occupy our time. On the surface, it's a classic argument against late capitalism and the societal harm of work for work's sake. Beneath the surface, Graeber unpicks a lot of threads that need unpicking around the subjects of self-worth, autonomy and how people are managed. A study published in 2021 entitled 'Alienation is not "bullshit": An empirical critique of Graeber's theory of BS jobs' (Magdalena et al, 2021), which challenged Graeber's key assertions, found that people who hate their jobs don't necessarily hate them because the work was inherently pointless, but because of their own lack of autonomy.

The study's authors argued that over-management, or micro-management, contributes to an employee's sense that their job is useless. And, of course, anyone who has been micro-managed has had to stop themselves saying 'Why don't you just do it yourself then?' to an over-eager boss. The rapid pivot to remote working many of us experienced in early 2020 put a natural stop on micro-management and people started to flourish. In a 2021 article for the *Financial Times*, the work and careers columnist Emma Jacobs argues that the battle between people who want workforces back in offices and people who want to work from where they like is a 'battle for autonomy'. She quotes a flexible work consultant who argues, 'If you strip away why people want flexibility, you find they want control over how much, where and when they work.'

As already mentioned, once employees get a taste for a better way of working, it's hugely risky to threaten to take it away. It's one thing for an employer to refuse to improve a worker's conditions. It's quite another thing for them to take away an improvement they've already got used to, whether it's increased choice of where to work or increased autonomy.

The hidden health obstacles overcome by remote working

While interviewing people for this book, we focused a lot of our attention on the benefits to their productivity and general happiness. A surprising theme emerged in a number of interviews. Regardless of their preference for remote work or office work, a lot of people value the opportunity to not show up to the office when their body tells them not to. A freelance accessibility consultant we spoke to revealed that, although she was self-employed, her role normally required her to be on-site with clients to do her job. She switched to working remotely almost without a hitch, using many of the same tools as everyone else, as well as a tool called UserZoom. Before her clients closed their offices, she'd attend user testing sessions to identify flaws in their products. The best way to do this was – and remains – to sit and watch users completing tasks, such as filling out a form or re-setting their password. Her role was to observe, moderate and report her findings, especially those related to accessibility of technology and software, to the clients. Without the opportunity to do in-person moderation, she relied almost entirely on remote moderation via UserZoom. She explained that there had been times in the past where she'd dreaded going into an office due to what she described as mild but inconvenient digestive issues. It was the sort of problem that wouldn't stop her working effectively, but it would make being in an office environment inconvenient.

Another person described to us their troubles with the skin condition psoriasis. 'It's basically chronic inflammation and I have a relatively mild form that is manageable 70 per cent of the time. When it flares up, I need to use a topical treatment to calm the irritation. There have been times where I've had to go to work wearing a thick skin cream that smells of petrol and leaves marks on my clothes. I would have been so much kinder to myself if I'd just worked from home, but it simply wasn't a thing at the time. So I could either call in sick or go in, feeling uncomfortable and self-conscious. My company has already switched to remote work for anyone who wants it so I can just deal with it when I need to without any hassle.'

Freelance journalist Rachael Reeves wrote powerfully about the problems many women typically face every month due to working from an office. 'Having a period may not be one of the reasons for me going freelance, but it has definitely been a top reason for staying so. I was fed up of going into office toilets and trying to curl up in a ball on the floor. It was unhygienic for a start. Now so many people are working from home, they can feel the same freedom as I do, to stretch out on the floor, switch the kettle on and turn off their Zoom camera. Yet, we are still there. It's better that your period has the biggest impact in the evening or at the weekend so it doesn't affect how your colleagues may view your work ethic' (Reeves, 2020).

The obvious advantages and disadvantages of remote working have been well discussed. The discourse has focused variously around culture, productivity and, to an extent, social affairs. It's harder to measure and discuss the private reasons why people have a preference, such as health matters or their personal living situation. During the first pandemic lockdown a number of organizations set up schemes to support people experiencing or at risk of experiencing domestic violence. For example, the Co-operative Bank commendably set out a plan very early on to ensure that people who didn't want to be at home for extended periods could still safely use a desk in one of their offices. Priority was given to people who were dealing with domestic violence.

To what extent is your home a place of work?

Working remotely is, of course, very likely to involve working at home. Even if you commit to using coffee shops and co-working spaces (or luxury hotels and business class air travel like Rowling and Shankman respectively), there's a very good chance you'll end up answering your phone or sending an email in the kitchen. Does that mean your home is a place of work, with all of the attendant requirements? There's already an enormous grey cloud of confusion looming over the distinctions between 'working from home' and 'living at work'. For every new freedom the remote worker experiences – walking the dog when they feel like it, sleeping in until five minutes before they clock on or showering on their lunch break – there are an equal number of potential corporate and organizational invasions. These will most likely come in two distinct flavours: corporate surveillance, and health and safety.

During the early weeks of the first pandemic lockdown, a friend of ours circulated a screenshot of a page from his mandatory workplace training. The content on the page instructed him to make a note of his nearest fire escape and to ensure it was free from obstruction. Alongside the screenshot, he shared a photograph of his bedroom window, obscured by two giant computer monitors in the foreground. This was his nearest fire escape because he was working from his bedroom. He'd recently started a new role working in the marketing team at a high street bank. The bank, being a bank, needed him to complete a range of modules on risk, fraud, regulatory compliance, ethics, information security and, of course, health and safety. The material he'd been asked to complete had been updated to reflect the new challenges of working from home and someone had obviously decided that even though most workers were in their own homes, they needed to demonstrate that they knew where their nearest fire escape was.

Did that person have a point? There's certainly no harm in reminding employees that you want them to be safe while working from home. The worst that can happen is that an employee might feel a little patronized and will try to make a meme out of it.

Yet it's quite plausible that employers will be held accountable for workplace accidents that happen outside of the workplace. If it can be proven that the accident was a result of their negligence then, of course, the lawyers will get involved and, to be fair, that's probably a good thing. In fact, research from National Accident Helpline has found that almost half of workers have had an accident or suffered an injury while working from home. The most common were back injuries caused by extended periods of sitting incorrectly (National Accident Helpline, 2021). Employers should absolutely make reasonable adjustments to help people work from home more safely. That can mean anything from supplying them with information on how to avoid back pain to buying them a fancy and expensive desk chair. If they fail to do this, and people suffer, it's right that they face any legal consequences.

In fact, in the UK, its health and safety regulator the Health and Safety Executive (HSE) published detailed guidance on its website about this very matter. The guidance covered a range of topics, from helping workers to understand the safest way to sit while using their computers, to helping them to avoid feelings of isolation and loneliness while adjusting to working alone and outside of their normal teams. The culture of health and safety in the UK has traditionally drawn ridicule, especially from elements of the right wing media, but this is genuinely important stuff.

But where do we draw the line between corporate governance and corporate overreach as it relates to people working outside of the traditional workplace? In September 2021 Bloomberg reported that Japan's largest brokerage firm, Nomura, had told its employees not to smoke at home during working hours. In a statement, the company said, 'There needs to be an environment in which everyone is healthy and can live lively in order for employees to fully demonstrate their ability, characters' (Nakamichi and Taniguchi, 2021). The company also conceded that its policy was practically unenforceable, but that it wanted to encourage healthy habits in its workers. If there was ever anything to make working from home objectively worse than working from an office for people who really didn't like working in offices in the first place, it's this sort of thing.

Your home may be monitored for quality and training purposes

A YouGov poll by employee compliance consultancy Skillcast found that 46 per cent of companies plan to implement some sort of health and wellbeing monitoring system for remote workers. This is one of those things that on paper seems entirely benevolent but has the potential for immense and rapid mission creep.

As well as invading their personal lives, some organizations are extending their use of workplace monitoring tools to compensate for their lack of physical proximity to their employees. A poll conducted by Opinium on behalf of the Prospect trade union found that a quarter of employees had been 'spied on' by their bosses during lockdown (Prospect, 2021). The research found that 23 per cent of people said their employer used technology to monitor them. Nine per cent said their bosses used cameras to keep tabs on them and 5 per cent said their employer was using keystroke logging. Take the poll with a pinch of salt, of course – it didn't appear to indicate whether these figures were an increase on tracking during normal times – but it's still not great reading. The YouGov poll for Skillcast found similar trends emerging (Dodd, 2020). Their research found that 12 per cent of all firms introduced remote tracking for people working outside of the office, with larger firms significantly more likely to want to track their staff.

And what happens when staff know they're being tracked? They adopt unhealthy working practices, and become anxious and suspicious of their bosses. A poll of 2,000 full-time workers conducted by cyber security firm Kaspersky found that 46 per cent of workers stayed logged in to work devices for longer than their contracted hours required due to being monitored by their employers (Brown, 2021). The operative phrase here is 'logged in'. The study didn't say whether the employees were working. David Emm, a Kaspersky spokesperson, said of the research that employers engaging in excessive surveillance were driving their employees into adopting unhealthy work behaviours in a bid to 'keep up appearances'. We explored how escaping the office potentially liberated workers from the 'competitive productivity' habits that offices foster. This sort of corporate overreach could actually lead to more competitive productivity, less effectiveness and – perhaps the most unintended consequence of all – drive workers to use personal devices for work in order to evade the gaze of their employer. Emm warned that employees 'using non-sanctioned personal devices for work tasks increases the vulnerability of corporate data and assets to hackers.'

Employers that want a remote workforce, and those that have been handed one for reasons they can't control, very quickly need to decide how they feel about autonomy and how much they trust their workforce. If installing keystroke tracking technology on an employee's machine is the answer, the employer is asking the wrong questions.

As the white-collar world gets to grips with the productivity and social implications of remote work, concerns around employee privacy have been somewhat overlooked. James Medd, a senior UX designer working in the north of England, explained to us that he was quite content with remote working, but absolutely hated 'effectively inviting colleagues and customers into my home when on video calls'. These are things organizations will need to iron out.

Ironing out some working practice kinks is one thing, but to some workers, remote monitoring is already becoming a dystopian nightmare. Imagine you're a customer service executive working from home, typing away at your computer. You're not on a call but your headset is on, and, without warning or invitation, or even knowing it was technically possible, you hear your boss's voice, guiding you through the task you're trying to complete. That's what happened to 'David', who spoke to the *Washington Post* on condition that he didn't give his full name (Abril and Harwell, 2021). To say he was surprised to learn that his boss could see what he was doing on his computer would be an understatement. This intrusion from his employer caused David an understandable amount of anxiety about his privacy. It affected his family. David's wife told the *Washington Post*, 'I was upstairs with my boys, and I get a text from my husband [David] that said, "If you come down here, don't say anything and let me know because we're being listened to".' David quit his job soon after this experience.

'It's just this constant, unnecessary, nerve-racking stress,' explained Kerrie Krutchik, a lawyer of 34 years experience, in the same interview with the *Washington Post*. 'You're trying to concentrate and in the back of your mind you know you're on camera the entire time,' she said. 'While you're reviewing a document, you don't know who is reviewing you.' As part of her remote working contract, Krutchik had consented to being tracked by facial recognition technology to monitor her productivity. She quit after two weeks.

'Ashley', another subject of corporate surveillance who spoke to the *Washington Post* on condition of anonymity, explained that she'd been furloughed by her employer, a banking startup, because she'd refused to give her consent to being tracked by a piece of software called Hubstaff. The software, which the makers describe on their website as a type of productivity tool, is able to take screenshots of an employee's screen at random intervals and record keystrokes, among other things. Ashley explained that it was an intrusion too far for her. 'I have so much information on my computer: my banking information, my passwords, my email that has stuff from my doctors,' she told reporters. 'I just wouldn't want my employers to have access to this.'

Ashley's employer was using surveillance to measure productivity. It had set an arbitrary acceptable activity level of 85 per cent, based on keystrokes and mouse movements. Ashley and her colleagues figured out that if they messaged each other more on the company's internal system, the tracking software would interpret that as 'productivity'. So that's what they did. The upshot of this workaround was that Ashley and her colleagues had stopped doing something very important. They were no longer taking time to think about their work and how to solve problems. Ashley told the *Washington Post* that 'people just stopped caring'.

Examples like David's, Kerrie's and Ashley's are bad for lots of reasons. Not least because they make workers sceptical of legitimate information security measures that could be the difference between a role going remote or not. Facial recognition software, for example, isn't new to most of us. Anyone with an iPhone newer than 2017's iPhone X has already agreed to pay for the privilege of giving one of the biggest corporations in the world access to their face and retinas. It's not the tech per se that's the problem, it's the motive for using it and the manner in which the data is handled. Lawyers, for example, need enhanced security to access certain very sensitive documents. In an office context, they engage with that enhanced security when they swipe into the building and again when they log on to their machine. From home, they need to compromise. And facial recognition technology is one way of doing that.

The problems start when employers take consent for things like enhanced security and treat it as an invitation to use that same technology to intrude into other areas, compromising their workers' privacy. The problems get substantially worse when these novel uses expose the limitations of the technology itself. Facial recognition technology may be useful for identifying you, but it's not necessarily any good at telling your boss whether you're working or not. Attorneys who spoke to the *Washington Post* agreed. 'The facial recognition systems, they said, felt intrusive, dysfunctional or annoying, booting them out of their work software if they shifted in their seat, rested their eyes, adjusted their glasses, wore a headband or necklace, went to the bathroom or had a child walk through their room' (Abril and Harwell, 2021).

The biggest mistake organizations will make as they transition to a hybrid model is trying to transplant their office culture into people's houses.

The decline of the middle manager

'More companies are exploring automation technologies, and more companies are rapidly digitising their businesses,' said André Dua, senior partner at McKinsey, in an interview with the *Guardian* (Issa, 2020). Dua paints a potentially grim picture for many jobs, concluding that what started out as an experiment driven by necessity has taught businesses that 'their work can be performed with anywhere from 5 per cent–25 per cent fewer employees'.

It's a common assumption that it will always be low-skill, high-effort jobs that die first at the hands of automation, with AI working its way steadily up the skills ladder, killing off ever more prestigious knowledge-based occupations. When it comes to the impact of AI, it's often a mistake to presume the things we're worried about are something that's about to happen in the near future. The things that worry us most are quite often already happening. Consider the print media. Before the digital age, this industry provided many blue-collar jobs: typesetters, printing press operators, delivery drivers and warehouse workers, to name a few. In the digital age, those blue-collar occupations have been replaced by white collar ones. Most of the printing presses that haven't become redundant due to the publications they produced moving online have been digitized. Delivery drivers still deliver papers, but in far smaller volumes. The same is true for warehouse workers serving the industry. And as for the higher-prestige role of the typesetter, it's best explained in a 2011 article entitled 'The day the typesetting industry died': 'The 1984 Macintosh was an interesting typographic tool but the 1985 combination with the Linotype type library and Adobe's PostScript changed the typographic world'. That's the opinion of Frank Romano, a print industry veteran and former editor of *Pocket Pal*, the definitive graphic arts handbook published by the International Paper Company.

In the article, Romano explained how he foresaw the end of the line for the traditional typesetter. 'I was sitting at the Spring 1985 introduction of what was called "Desktop Publishing." Paul Brainerd of Aldus had coined the term and his Pagemaker program allowed page makeup on a screen. The 300 dpi Laserwriter and the 1200 dpi Linotype Linotron imagesetter brought it all into a system.' Romano continued: 'Pretty soon graphic designers were composing pages with type. They could select fonts and sizes and formats, and without realizing it, were bypassing the typesetting services. The same designers who attacked proofs with a plethora of changes suddenly lowered their standards. Over time, quality was automated into QuarkXPress and Adobe InDesign.'

We're subject to powerful biases when we contemplate the impact of AI and automation. A 2017 study by the Pew Research Center found that most Americans accept that automation will have a profound effect on the future of work. On the whole, the study found that Americans foresee a future 'in which robots and computers have moved beyond performing repeated or routine tasks and are now capable of performing most of the jobs that are currently done by humans'. The study also found 'a significant majority of today's workers express little concern that their own jobs or careers might be performed by machines in their lifetimes'. A 2019 study conducted by software company SAP and experience management company Qualtrics and was presented to the World Economic Forum found – again – that while most people accept the plausibility of automation making a large number of jobs obsolete, when it comes to their own job, 80 per cent of the world's workers believe that it could only be performed by a human (SAP and Qualtrics, 2019). Interestingly, confidence about one's own replaceability varies massively by geography. 'By and large, participants from Europe and Central Asia were the most confident that their jobs require a human touch, as those regions had the lowest percentages of people saying that technology could do "most of" or "almost all of" what they do in their current jobs. On the other end of the spectrum, 30 percent of participants from South Asia felt entirely replaceable by existing technology, and another 19 percent said that most of their job responsibilities could be automated' (Futurism, 2019). We're all pragmatists when it comes to other people's jobs.

In the 2020 book *The Coming of Neo-Feudalism: A warning to the global middle class*, author and software engineer Joel Kotkin sounds an alarm bell to the middle managers of the world. While most of our concern about automation and jobs appears reserved for people in jobs that are routine and fairly low prestige, Kotkin sees things differently. He believes that organizational trends suggest that, eventually, the world will be able to pretty well do without middle managers. It's something he's seen for himself working for large IT firms. 'The people running today's IT firms do not see middle managers – much less assembly-line workers or skilled artisans – as peers' (Kotkin, 2020).

Thinking about the algorithmically driven future of distributed work-forces, Kotkin predicts that the requirement for middle management will be on the wane. 'A technologically driven society tends to show a widening gap between the "elect" who are highly gifted in science and tech, and the many who are not. Today it takes only a small cadre of coders, financial experts, and marketing mavens to build a billion-dollar business, without much required in the way of blue-collar workers or even middle managers.'

Rachel, who we've heard from throughout this book, believes that as well as technological advances, the increase in documentation and project tracking reduces the need for some of the skills we associate with middle managers. 'Working from home during lockdown, I wonder if there's a bit of a crisis for middle managers. If we can move to a space where work tasks are documented, tracked and evaluated using software like Jira, Trello and Slack, then what's their purpose? In theory, this software should allow employees to work in a more autonomous and flexible way. So it feels pretty redundant to have these middle managers: people who don't deliver things or make the major decisions.'

Remote working is already helping organizations identify new sources of efficiency. But the practice is also ruthlessly exposing existing and longstanding inefficiencies. While both are positive when it comes to the bottom line, organizations must be careful not to conflate 'inefficient' with 'redundant'. As businesses get busy reducing their office overheads, policy makers and pundits are rightly worried that their next move will be to take the axe to staff over-heads. The Tony Blair Institute for Change study we cited in the first chapter estimated a potential loss of six million white collar UK jobs (Kakkad, 2021). The theory being that if it can be done remotely, it can be done offshore.

Remote working is not an excuse for a ruthless culling of jobs – and, more importantly, the people that hold them – because organizations are experiencing a momentary sugar high from their newfound love of optimized efficiency. Certain marginalized groups stand to suffer most when businesses go on efficiency drives. 'Women are overrepresented in automation-risky jobs, such as secretaries and retail workers,' says Dr Niki Vincent, Commissioner for Equal Opportunity in South Australia (Issa, 2020). Dr Vincent sees a shift toward less automatable jobs as a partial solution here, arguing that 'there are still not enough women choosing to study things like engineering or coding'. However, although it is true that women are underrepresented in engineering and software development, 'learn to code' isn't a comprehensive enough solution to the risks faced.

Conclusion

We're grateful to everyone who has taken the time to share their insights and expertise with us for this book. It has been a privilege to get what felt like a front-row seat to observe people adjusting to one of the biggest industrial and economic disruptions in recent memory. People have been exceptionally generous with their insights and wisdom. We've been struck by the diversity of opinion and experience. No two remote working experiences have been the same and the points of difference have often been profound.

We're also grateful to the institutions that have been researching the various effects of remote working on things like organizational health, productivity and wellbeing. Without their insights this book would have been a little too heavy on opinion and speculation. But the most interesting and revealing themes we've gleaned have more often than not come from the casual observations and half-formulated ideas of the working people we've been speaking to. The deeply and expensively researched studies we've cited have been extremely useful from a quantitative point of view, but you can't beat a chat with someone who is experiencing the transition to hybrid or remote working in real time.

Take Nathan and David's reaction to noticing how strongly their workplace smelled when they returned. Both said it had a noticeable impact on their mood. We're willing to bet that not many employers have put much thought into how their workplace smells and the impact this might have on their workforce. They'll quite probably have been too busy thinking about the space between desks and how best to implement a one-way system to contemplate it.

Consider Zorica's habit of making social plans that bookend her workday so that she can't fall into the trap of over-work as another example. From one perspective, it's a personal solution to a problem she'd identified in her own working life. But her employer, or any employer, could – and should – take it and run with it. It's all very well discouraging over-work, but Zorica came to the party with a concrete, actionable plan to combat it. And her plan had a measurable improvement on the satisfaction she experienced both professionally and personally.

Steph, the consultant who cottoned on to a colleague's penchant for passive-aggressive appointment setting, raised an extremely interesting point about communication habits in the remote working world. Rachel, the government employee, highlighted issues with her employer's tendency to transpose office-based working practices into remote settings and the potentially underappreciated benefits of remote working to natural introverts. Ross, the energy auditor, illuminated to us the risks and challenges faced by natural extroverts.

These unique observations and insights should be treated as jumping off points for any reader now contemplating how best to build or contribute to a remote work culture within their own organization. Hopefully we've communicated sufficiently our optimism for remote working and its immense potential to improve job satisfaction, work–life balance (or, more accurately, work–life integration), productivity and happiness. And hopefully we've balanced that with a measured assessment of the downsides, of which many are very significant.

The 2020 report by McKinsey we cited earlier analysed comparative productivity when people performed certain tasks remotely and from an office. The report found that 'finance and insurance has the highest potential, with three-quarters of time spent on activities that can be done remotely without a loss of productivity'. Unsurprisingly, agriculture, accommodation, construction, transportation and warehousing, mining and retail were occupations with the lowest potential for remote work. This tells us that remote working is inherently inequitable. It benefits some more significantly than others.

In fact, the most important thing we've learned from writing and researching this book is that there are numerous inherent yet extremely well hidden inequalities baked into all working environments, whether that's the office, the home or the third workplace. The role of remote culture as we see it is to bring about as much workplace justice as possible, to attenuate the impact of these baked-in inequalities and where possible, to help organizations and their people collaborate to overcome them. Establishing healthy remote cultures will be a balancing act.

Well-structured and well-managed hybrid working policies will evolve to support people through differing phases in life where they have different personal and professional requirements. We anticipate that in most sectors young workers will gravitate to the office when it suits them and gravitate away from it when it doesn't. They'll naturally need more support and guidance early in their working lives. Offices will continue to be a good place for lots of people. Instead of mandating minimum attendance at the office, organizations should trust all of their staff to know when to, and when not to, lean into the office environment. People used to come into their office because that's what was expected. We're hoping this will no longer be the case and workers will come into the office when the office is the right place to be.

There are lots of reasons why the office might be the right place to be for any given time. Sometimes workers will feel the need for additional support, they'll want specific training or mentorship and sometimes they'll simply want a change of scenery. The same will be true for the home and the third workplace. There will be phases in some people's careers where they spend prolonged periods of time in one of the three main settings. Again, the drivers behind these choices are diverse and not easy to predict. Nor should they necessarily need to be made public. Employees may elect to work from home because of health issues, emotional problems, caring obligations, or a simple desire to escape the mire of workplace politics and focus on deep work. Averaged out over years and then decades, workers may split their time roughly equally between office, home and 'third workplace'. But these phases won't be split into equal chunks spread neatly across the working week.

Most organizations see remote working as a compromise. That's fine. Most employees see having to go into an office as a compromise too. Hybrid working might represent the sweet spot in the middle of these two arrangements, but that doesn't mean it represents a best of both worlds scenario where the employer gets the best end of the deal for 2.5 days a week and the employee gets the spoils for the other half. We predict that, for most people, hybrid working will evolve from what it is now – an experiment where both parties agree to share the risk on what are often fairly rigid terms – into a set of policies and agreements, both formal and informal, that are focused exclusively on fostering as much flexibility as possible.

Anyone with any influence over their organization's culture should be looking to harness the flexibility that remote work promises to achieve long-lasting, sustainable improvements for everyone. Remote working can remove barriers to access for disabled people. It can make jobs more accessible to people who can't afford to relocate and to people who simply do not want to move away from family. It has the capacity to redistribute wealth and prosperity, to decentralize the economy, to support more rewarding careers, make us better at our jobs and deliver more quality time to workers and their families.

The chances of society abandoning remote work and returning to a culture of office-centricity are almost nil. For that to happen, we'd not only need to undo every bit of progress achieved since the Covid-19 pandemic, we'd need to convince those who'd adopted remote working years beforehand that they were wrong and that the commercial real estate owners, coffee chains and politicians with vested interests were right. It's very unlikely to happen. The worst thing we could do is treat remoteness as something to be overcome, competed against and proven wrong. But this doesn't mean remote working is automatically destined to be a resounding success. Nor does it mean remote work should get a free pass and become the de facto way of working without due scrutiny and challenge. We've got a great tradition of critiquing office culture and we should devote the same energy to remote culture.

REFERENCES

Introduction

Groves, J (2021) Get back to work! Furious bosses condemn Whitehall blueprint to give workers the right to work from home forever and make it *illegal* to force them back to the office, *Daily Mail*, 16 June. www.dailymail.co.uk/news/article-9694403/Shock-plans-work-home-forever-Ministers-propose-make-illegal-forced-office.html (archived at https://perma.cc/ECY8-6NBE)

Kakkad, J, Palmou, C, Britto, D and Browne, J (2021) Anywhere jobs: Reshaping the geography of work, Tony Blair Institute for Global Change, 16 June. https://institute.global/policy/anywhere-jobs-reshaping-geography-work (archived at https://perma.cc/6UMW-YBDT)

Kelly, J (2020) Americans are excessively eating, drinking, smoking pot, playing video games and watching porn while quarantined, *Forbes*, 6 April. www.forbes.com/sites/jackkelly/2020/04/06/americans-are-excessively-eating-drinking-smoking-pot-playing-video-games-and-watching-porn-while-quarantined/ (archived at https://perma.cc/A5ZV-A4C2)

Louise, N (2019) Remote surgery: Doctor uses robot to perform first long-distance heart surgery, Tech Startups, 03/10. https://techstartups.com/2019/10/03/remote-surgery-doctor-uses-robot-perform-first-long-distance-heart-surgery/ (archived at https://perma.cc/JV3H-WJQK)

Lutke, T (2020) As of today, Shopify is a digital by default company. We will keep our offices closed until 2021 so that we can rework them for this new reality. And after that, most will permanently work remotely. Office centricity is over. [Twitter] 21 May. https://twitter.com/tobi/status/1263483496087064579 (archived at https://perma.cc/K5ES-VCT5)

Packard, J and Thomas, D (2021) UK ministers reject post-Covid right to work from home, *Financial Times*, 17 June. www.ft.com/content/49ea21b6-12d6-49bc-955a-19abbd928b76 (archived at https://perma.cc/UYB7-DFUT)

Patel, T, Shah, S and Pancholy, S (2019) Long distance tele-robotic-assisted percutaneous coronary intervention: A report of first-in-human experience, *The Lancet*, 3 September. www.thelancet.com/journals/eclinm/article/PIIS2589-5370(19)30137-3/fulltext (archived at https://perma.cc/GT2V-4XCZ)

Samanti, H (2021) Address not applicable: What happens to the HQ in the remote-work age? The Real Deal, 1 March. https://therealdeal.com/2021/03/01/address-not-applicable-what-happens-to-the-hq-in-the-remote-work-age/ (archived at https://perma.cc/D7QY-W63R)

Chapter 1

Jaques, E (1951) *The Changing Culture of a Factory*, Tavistock Publications in collaboration with Routledge, Oxford

Chapter 2

BBC (2020) Dimitar Berbatov: Lazy? No, I was smart, says ex-Tottenham and Man Utd striker, BBC, 3 May. www.bbc.co.uk/sport/football/52511238 (archived at https://perma.cc/D8MF-K62L)

BBC Radio 5Live (2020) People are getting lazy Pupils are going back to school and now the government is launching a new ad campaign, pushing workers to get back into the office. Adalat owns a coffee shop in London, he told @ NickyAACampbell, its about time. [Twitter] 1 September. https://mobile.twitter.com/bbc5live/status/1300692231511248896 (archived at https://perma.cc/8NZB-JEYQ)

Bragg, J (2011) Lazy footballers – Berbatov, Bendtner, Taarabt, Lineker and more, Talk Sport. 27 July. https://talksport.com/uncategorized/113960/lazy-footballers-berbatov-bendtner-taarabt-lineker-and-more/ (archived at https://perma.cc/AAS4-ZGLR)

British Council for Offices and Savills (2016) *What Workers Want*, June 2016. https://pdf.savills.com/documents/What_Workers_Want_2016.pdf (archived at https://perma.cc/EBN2-ESXL)

Carter, A (2021) Older workers planning to work from home permanently are selfishly risking the development of young people, *CityAM*, 23 June. www.cityam.com/older-workers-planning-to-work-from-home-permanently-are-selfishly-risking-the-development-of-young-people/ (archived at https://perma.cc/5M69-NPRD)

Clason, G S (1926) *The Richest Man in Babylon*, Penguin, London

Costa, M (2021) 'Your career doesn't have to be your entire life': Why some companies are encouraging side hustles, Digiday, 20 September. https://digiday.com/marketing/your-career-doesnt-have-to-be-your-entire-life-why-some-companies-are-encouraging-side-hustles/ (archived at https://perma.cc/BDM5-UYSE)

Cotton, B (2021) What is the value of UK's 'Side Hustle' economy? Business Leader, 20 September. www.businessleader.co.uk/what-is-the-value-of-uks-side-hustle-economy/ (archived at https://perma.cc/4FH7-ZKHU)

De Fraja, G, Matheson, J and Rockey, J (2021) Zoomshock: The geography and local labour market consequences of working from home, *Covid Economics*, 13 January 2021, **64**, 1–41. https://ssrn.com/abstract=3752977 (archived at https://perma.cc/KT2Q-ZBNB)

Dhawan, E (2021) Why the hybrid workforce of the future depends on the 'geriatric millennial', Medium, 22 April. https://index.medium.com/why-the-hybrid-workforce-of-the-future-depends-on-the-geriatric-millennial-6f9ff4d e1d23 (archived at https://perma.cc/8KMF-BU2H)

Duncan Smith, Sir I (2021) In the 1940s they kept coming to the office – even when Hitler's bombs were raining down, Daily Mail, 9 October. www.dailymail.co.uk/debate/article-10076329/SIR-IAIN-DUNCAN-SMITH-1940s-kept-coming-office-bombs-came-down.html (archived at https://perma.cc/H22J-M8UJ)

Frith, B (2016) Over-ambitious workers make others insecure, HR Magazine, 22 April. www.hrmagazine.co.uk/content/news/over-ambitious-workers-make-others-insecure (archived at https://perma.cc/8NZB-JEYQ)

Hatton, B (2021) Go back to office to get on in careers, Sunak urges young people, Independent, 2 August. www.independent.co.uk/news/business/news/rishi-sunak-young-people-office-b1895525.html (archived at https://perma.cc/9YG8-66SE)

Jacobs, E (2021) Arup's seven-day week: Is this the future of work? Financial Times, 11 October. www.ft.com/content/1405cb93-6625-4834-ac07-09e4062e7aa7 (archived at https://perma.cc/988K-GRH2)

Kiwi Movers (2017) Hammocks and ping pong tables going into storage: Is this the end of the 'fun' startup office? Kiwi Movers, 15 July. www.kiwimovers.co.uk/news/hammocks-and-ping-pong-tables-going-into-storage-is-this-end-of-the-fun-startup-office/ (archived at https://perma.cc/9V95-AQ9G)

Klosk, R (2020) Measuring productivity in remote workforces, Forbes, 20 August. www.forbes.com/sites/forbeshumanresourcescouncil/2020/08/20/measuring-productivity-in-remote-workforces/ (archived at https://perma.cc/2TEF-5C4H)

Kochar, A (2021) Remote work vacancies in the UK up by 452% ,Think Remote, 12 August. https://thinkremote.com/remote-work-vacancies-in-the-uk-up-by-452/ (archived at https://perma.cc/3KZV-2XDT)

Line, H (2021) Cut pay for working at home: Minister wants to slash wages of civil servants who have not returned to the office since Covid restrictions were lifted, Daily Mail, 8 August. www.dailymail.co.uk/news/article-9874691/Minister-wants-slash-wages-civil-servants-not-returned-office.html (archived at https://perma.cc/4Z2K-FER3)

Love Money (2020) From Slack to Instagram, massive companies that started as side hustles, Love Money, 20 September. www.lovemoney.com/galleries/68770/massive-companies-started-side-hustles-slack-instagram?page=1 (archived at https://perma.cc/8YXS-JMPE)

Lytton, C (2021) The double income was too good to pass up: Meet the white collar workers with two full-time jobs, Telegraph, 13/10. www.telegraph.co.uk/education-and-careers/2021/10/13/double-income-good-pass-meet-white-collar-workers-two-full-time/ (archived at https://perma.cc/BQ36-G4JB)

Meister, J C (2019) Survey: What employees want most from their workspaces, *Harvard Business Review*, 26 August. https://hbr.org/2019/08/survey-what-employees-want-most-from-their-workspaces (archived at https://perma.cc/Y7VK-VERL)

Mikhailova, A and Owen, G (2021) People were left to the Taliban who could have been saved: Ministers' fury that, with four out of five working from home, civil servants couldn't access secret documents and wasted critical days during Afghan exit as UK citizens, *Daily Mail*, 9 October. www.dailymail.co.uk/news/article-10076061/Home-working-left-Britons-Talibans-mercy-Afghanistan-Ministers-claim.html (archived at https://perma.cc/KYZ5-KR6P)

O'Donovan, C (2021) Stitch Fix took away flexible scheduling for employees. Hundreds of them just quit, Buzzfeed News, 19 August. www.buzzfeednews.com/article/carolineodonovan/stitch-fix-employees-quitting (archived at https://perma.cc/UBV5-BVHZ)

Peters, A (2015) At this office, the break room is a giant ball pit, *Fast Company*, 2 September. www.fastcompany.com/3041903/at-this-office-the-break-room-is-a-giant-ball-pit (archived at https://perma.cc/2A7P-PLCG)

Riach, D (2017) I was a multi-millionaire by 27 – here's what I learned, CNBC, 28 March. www.cnbc.com/2017/03/28/i-was-a-multi-millionaire-by-27-heres-what-i-learned.html (archived at https://perma.cc/L6GG-RQQM)

Rosekind, M R, Gregory, K B, Mallis, M M, Brandt, S L, Seal, B and Lerner, D (2010) The cost of poor sleep: Workplace productivity loss and associated costs, National Library of Medicine. https://pubmed.ncbi.nlm.nih.gov/20042880/ (archived at https://perma.cc/X9UQ-6C5B)

Roue, L (2017) Salford boss turns office into giant ball pool, *Manchester Evening News*, 6 May. www.manchestereveningnews.co.uk/business/business-news/salford-boss-turns-office-giant-12991704 (archived at https://perma.cc/LZG8-U4UH)

Smith, A (2020) Premier League running stats this season revealed, Sky Sports, 28 May. www.skysports.com/football/news/11661/11996016/premier-league-running-stats-this-season-revealed (archived at https://perma.cc/RGN5-LMBP)

Sugar, Lord A (2021) Boris says it's no longer necessary to work from home. So city people get back to the offices let's kick start the local economy for shops, cafes who suffered badly. Some people may have become complacent liking this new style of working. Well those folk will never work for me. [Twitter] 5 July. https://twitter.com/lord_sugar/status/1412100387264471043 (archived at https://perma.cc/JDZ5-3VMA)

Chapter 3

Bayerischer Rundfunk (2021) Objective or biased: On the questionable use of artificial intelligence for job applications. https://interaktiv.br.de/ki-bewerbung/en/ (archived at https://perma.cc/27T2-Y7PK)

Dean, B (2021) Fiverr usage and growth statistics: How many people use Fiverr in 2021? Backlinko, 20 April. https://backlinko.com/fiverr-users (archived at https://perma.cc/JMD4-QTZR)

Goodhart, D (2017) *The Road to Somewhere: The populist revolt and the future of politics*, C Hurst & Co Publishers Ltd, London

Herd, C (2021) Office: Hire best person in a 30-mile radius. Remote: Hire best person in the world. Office: $20,000 / worker / year. Remote: $1,500 / worker / year. Remote-first teams have already won. Twitter, 16 January. https://twitter.com/chris_herd/status/1286676040027443200 (archived at https://perma.cc/6NYX-JJ3X)

Kakkad, J, Palmou, C, Britto, D and Browne, J (2021) Anywhere jobs: Reshaping the geography of work, Tony Blair Institute for Global Change, 16 June. https://institute.global/policy/anywhere-jobs-reshaping-geography-work (archived at https://perma.cc/6UMW-YBDT)

Kalyan Maity, S, Bhanu Jha, C, Kumar, A, Sengupta, A, Modi, M and Animesh, M (2016) A large-scale analysis of the marketplace characteristics in Fiverr, Indian Institute of Technology Kharagpur, 20 September. https://arxiv.org/abs/1609.06004 (archived at https://perma.cc/878A-EJU4)

Massmann, O (2021) Vietnam: The rising digital economy – what you must know, Lexology, 1 March. www.lexology.com/library/detail.aspx?g=8f0883fa-7dcb-428c-a0ad-892bbe8d065d (archived at https://perma.cc/5JVJ-SA43)

Wilson, A (2020) Global responses to the new WFH era: From Tallinn to Ho Chi Minh City, people are adapting to the new normal of working from home. Here's the experience of five cities, Raconteur, 25 June. www.raconteur.net/global-business/global-cities-remote/ (archived at https://perma.cc/EKQ4-6DVA)

Chapter 4

Bernhard, A (2020) The great bicycle boom of 2020, BBC. www.bbc.com/future/bespoke/made-on-earth/the-great-bicycle-boom-of-2020.html (archived at https://perma.cc/FFW2-AQZN)

Cunliffe, R (2020) For young Londoners, working from home is a cramped and dismal experience, *CityAM*, 5 August. www.cityam.com/for-young-londoners-working-from-home-is-a-cramped-and-dismal-experience/ (archived at https://perma.cc/WZV5-YNZ7)

Department for Business, Energy and Industrial Strategy (2019) Business population estimates for the UK and regions: 2019 statistical release, 14 January. https://assets.publishing.service.gov.uk/government/uploads/system/uploads/attachment_data/file/852919/Business_Population_Estimates_for_the_UK_and_regions_-_2019_Statistical_Release.pdf (archived at https://perma.cc/WX46-WHSC)

Hoffower, H (2021) Remote work didn't wipe out big cities – it made them even bigger, Business Insider, 20 September. https://flipboard.com/@businessinsider/top-stories-qcjv43d7z/remote-work-didn-t-wipe-out-big-cities-it-made-them-even-bigger/a-aVe7kvtHRdOOpItUVnATVQ%3Aa%3A48159484-f83a967eef%2Fbusinessinsider.com (archived at https://perma.cc/D2WC-YMP7)

Hosking, P (2021) Staff 'will quit if companies force them back to their desks full-time', The Times, 17 July. www.thetimes.co.uk/article/staff-will-quit-if-companies-force-them-back-to-their-desks-full-time-nr0885xkx (archived at https://perma.cc/9G3F-U6D2)

Kimmage, P (2004) The big interview: Neil Webb, The Times, 28 November. https://www.thetimes.co.uk/article/the-big-interview-neil-webb-z2dtm20mt02 (archived at https://perma.cc/FV7R-GK4W)

Kotkin, J (2020) The Coming of Neo-Feudalism: A warning to the global middle class, Encounter Books, New York

McKinsey (2020) What's next for remote work: An analysis of 2,000 tasks, 800 jobs, and nine countries. www.mckinsey.com/featured-insights/future-of-work/whats-next-for-remote-work-an-analysis-of-2000-tasks-800-jobs-and-nine-countries (archived at https://perma.cc/4QWU-V9GY)

Partridge, J (2020) Google commits to vast London office despite rise of remote working, Guardian, 28 July. www.theguardian.com/technology/2020/jul/28/google-commits-to-vast-london-office-despite-rise-of-remote-working (archived at https://perma.cc/GK86-SVDT)

Pet Food Manufacturers' Association (nd) PFMA confirms dramatic rise in pet acquisition among millennials. www.pfma.org.uk/news/pfma-confirms-dramatic-rise-in-pet-acquisition-among-millennials- (archived at https://perma.cc/5QJA-CYHB)

Reid, C (2020) Bike sales increased 63% during lockdown, reveals UK's Bicycle Association, Forbes. www.forbes.com/sites/carltonreid/2020/08/03/bike-sales-increased-63-during-lockdown-reveals-uks-bicycle-association/?sh=3335b6b07e12 (archived at https://perma.cc/92FN-B2JV)

Talk Radio (2021) 'We need to unmuzzle ourselves and get back into our offices. It must be taking a toll on the nation's mental health.' Commentator Darren Grimes says working from home has to end. @mrmarkdolan | @darrengrimes_ | #talkRADIO [Twitter] https://twitter.com/talkradio/status/1412474677021360135?lang=en (archived at https://perma.cc/3C9E-GNQQ)

Waheed, J (2021) Alan Sugar blasted for tweet urging complacent people to return to office amid freedom day, *Metro*, 6 July. https://metro.co.uk/2021/07/06/lord-alan-sugar-blasted-for-tweet-urging-people-to-return-to-office-14879902/ (archived at https://perma.cc/PLH9-SM79)

Waugh, R (2019) Making sense of the knowledge economy, *Telegraph*, 23 April. www.telegraph.co.uk/business/tips-for-the-future/the-knowledge-economy/ (archived at https://perma.cc/LX3Z-HA52)

Willems, M (2021) London, Paris and New York: The cities that migrate faster to flexible working, *CityAM*, 2 October. www.cityam.com/london-paris-and-new-york-the-cities-that-migrate-faster-to-flexible-working/ (archived at https://perma.cc/H9RT-NWRS)

Chapter 5

Albarran, A (2021) Open offices failed. These are 6 essentials to make sure the next office doesn't, *Fast Company*, 10 June. www.fastcompany.com/90682289/open-offices-failed-workers-these-are-6-essentials-to-make-sure-future-offices-dont (archived at https://perma.cc/NJ6V-YGNT)

Belluck, P (2015) Chilly at work? Office formula was devised for men, *The New York Times*, 3 August. www.nytimes.com/2015/08/04/science/chilly-at-work-a-decades-old-formula-may-be-to-blame.html (archived at https://perma.cc/H237-NCAB)

Bernstein, E and Waber, B (2019) The truth about open offices, *Harvard Business Review*, November–December. https://hbr.org/2019/11/the-truth-about-open-offices (archived at https://perma.cc/NH9N-3CFJ)

Bryant, A (2017) Erika Nardini on the value of leading '10 percent' players, *The New York Times*, 14 July. www.nytimes.com/2017/07/14/business/erika-nardini-barstool-sports-value-of-leading-10-percent-players.html (archived at https://perma.cc/Z3NP-KUCW)

Gateley, B (2018) We tried unlimited holiday for three years. Here's everything that went wrong. Charlie HR. www.charliehr.com/blog/we-tried-unlimited-holiday-heres-everything-that-went-wrong/ (archived at https://perma.cc/TLS7-V92B)

Greenwood, G, Elison, A and Khan, S (2021) Colour coded lanyards let staff keep their distance, *The Times*, 13 August. www.thetimes.co.uk/article/colour-coded-lanyards-let-staff-keep-their-distance-x2lgtldvx (archived at https://perma.cc/MW84-PZE7)

Jones, P and Bano, N (2021) The right to disconnect, Autonomy, 16 August. https://autonomy.work/portfolio/righttodisconnect/ (archived at https://perma.cc/DQ9T-4GKJ)

Lewis, S and Cooper, C (2005) *Work–Life Integration: Case studies of organisational change*, Wiley, Hoboken, NJ

Meyersohn, N (2020) Acrylic glass shields are everywhere, but its not clear how much they help, CNN, 14 October. https://edition.cnn.com/2020/10/13/business/plexiglass-shields-coronavirus/index.html (archived at https://perma.cc/NS5N-ZYSY)

Murray, N (2020) *Burnout Britain: Overwork in an age of unemployment*, 4 Day Week Campaign, Compass and Autonomy. https://autonomy.work/wp-content/uploads/2020/10/4DW-mentalhealth_cumpass_4dwcORANGE_C-v2.pdf (archived at https://perma.cc/P552-FLRY)

Newport, C (2016) *Deep Work: Rules for focused success in a distracted world*, Grand Central Publishing, New York

Oldenburg, R (1989) *The Great Good Place: Cafes, coffee shops, bookstores, bars, hair salons, and other hangouts at the heart of a community*, 18 August, Da Capo Press, Boston

Peterson, G (2021) Want to work 9-to-5? Good luck building a career, *Fortune*, 17 August. https://fortune.com/2021/08/17/work-life-balance-9-to-5-jobs-career-building/ (archived at https://perma.cc/27N3-95T2)

Thompson, D (2020) Hygiene theater is a huge waste of time, *The Atlantic*, 27 July. www.theatlantic.com/ideas/archive/2020/07/scourge-hygiene-theater/614599/ (archived at https://perma.cc/V8ZA-HD99)

University of Exeter (2010) Designing your own workspace improves health, happiness and productivity, University of Exeter, 7 September. www.exeter.ac.uk/news/featurednews/title_98638_en.html (archived at https://perma.cc/E729-7RY4)

Yang, Maya (2020) Why 'unlimited' time off isn't actually unlimited, BBC Worklife, 10 January. www.bbc.com/worklife/article/20200108-is-minimum-leave-a-better-alternative-to-unlimited-time-off (archived at https://perma.cc/6Z8S-M4Q8)

Chapter 6

Bergen, M and Eidelson, J (2018) Inside Google's shadow workforce, Bloomberg, 25 July. www.bloomberg.com/news/articles/2018-07-25/inside-google-s-shadow-workforce (archived at https://perma.cc/5EV2-XVWU)

Carter, L (2016) Presenteeism costs economy $34 billion a year through lost productivity, report shows, ABC News, 12 April. www.abc.net.au/news/2016-04-12/presenteeism-costing-the-economy-billions/7318832 (archived at https://perma.cc/SD9M-3W3H)

Hall, A and Rowan, C (2021) Have you caught the 'super cold'? Here's how to tackle the symptoms, *Telegraph*, 28 October. www.telegraph.co.uk/health-fitness/body/super-cold-symptoms-have-you-caught-remedies-worst-cold-ever/ (archived at https://perma.cc/VG7P-3ZK5)

Heinemeier Hansson, D and Fried, J (2013) *Remote: Office not required*, Random House, New York

Office for National Statistics (2021) Labour market overview, UK: September 2021, 14 September. www.ons.gov.uk/employmentandlabourmarket/peoplein work/employmentandemployeetypes/bulletins/uklabourmarket/september2021 (archived at https://perma.cc/2MD6-A5W4)

Partridge, J (2020) Google commits to vast London office despite rise of remote working, *Guardian*, 28 July. www.theguardian.com/technology/2020/jul/28/ google-commits-to-vast-london-office-despite-rise-of-remote-working (archived at https://perma.cc/GK86-SVDT)

Peel, A (2020) Digital presenteeism, Digital People, 27 October. https://digitalpeople. blog.gov.uk/2020/10/27/digital-presenteeism/ (archived at https://perma.cc/ MUE8-8H8G)

World Economic Forum (2020) *Accelerating Digital Inclusion in the New Normal*, July. www3.weforum.org/docs/WEF_Accelerating_Digital_Inclusion_in_the_ New_Normal_Report_2020.pdf (archived at https://perma.cc/7YMW-QSTX)

Zitron, E (2021) Why managers fear a remote-work future, *The Atlantic*, 29 July. www.theatlantic.com/ideas/archive/2021/07/work-from-home-benefits/619597/ (archived at https://perma.cc/D87R-L6YA)

Chapter 7

Carter, T (2021) The true failure rate of small businesses, Entrepreneur Europe, 3 January. www.entrepreneur.com/article/361350 (archived at https://perma.cc/ K2EH-TQED)

Scottish Financial News (2020) Over 600,000 small UK businesses at risk of failure in 2020, 2 March. www.scottishfinancialnews.com/article/over-600-000-small-uk-businesses-at-risk-of-failure-in-2020 (archived at https://perma.cc/7T5Z-XDV4)

Chapter 8

Beck, K et al (nd) Manifesto for agile software development. https://agilemanifesto. org/ (archived at https://perma.cc/RB2N-X2SL)

Newport, C (2016) *Deep Work: Rules for focused success in a distracted world*, Piaktus, London.

Schaub, M (2016) Rowdy J K Rowling reveals 'graffiti-ing' of hotel statue after she finished *Harry Potter*, *Los Angeles Times*, www.latimes.com/books/jacketcopy/ la-et-jc-jk-rowling-rowdy-vandalized-hotel-20160112-story.html (archived at https://perma.cc/RC2D-2GLJ)

Shankman, P (2016) How I wrote 28,482 words on one flight, 30 August. www. shankman.com/wrote-28482-words-one-flight-yesterday/ (archived at https:// perma.cc/3RTM-SLE4)

Chapter 9

Brown, J (2021) Experts call for fewer video meetings as research identifies causes of Zoom fatigue, People Management, 2 March. www.peoplemanagement.co. uk/news/articles/experts-call-for-fewer-video-meetings-as-research-identifies-causes-of-zoom-fatigue (archived at https://perma.cc/X38X-TJUY)

Hill, A (2021) 'It's awkward': How UK workers hired remotely feel returning to the office, *Guardian*, 27 September. www.theguardian.com/money/2021/sep/27/ its-awkward-how-uk-workers-hired-remotely-feel-returning-to-the-office (archived at https://perma.cc/JPK6-DQC9)

Murphy Kelly, S (2021) Stop making employees turn on webcams during meetings, CNN, 24 September. https://edition.cnn.com/2021/09/24/tech/webcams-work place-meetings/index.html (archived at https://perma.cc/C759-D5WZ)

Shaw, Dougal (2020) Coronavirus: What's it like to start a new job when working remotely? BBC, 17 June. www.bbc.co.uk/news/business-52900325 (archived at https://perma.cc/68WL-FHLG)

Chapter 10

Abril, D and Harwell, D (2021) Keystroke tracking, screenshots, and facial recogni-tion: The boss may be watching long after the pandemic ends, *Washington Post*, 24 September. www.washingtonpost.com/technology/2021/09/24/remote-work-from-home-surveillance/ (archived at https://perma.cc/GZ4X-LP6P)

Bizley, N (2019) Sewage smells, rodents and shabby carpets: The UK workplace in 2019, *The HR Director*, 11 June. www.thehrdirector.com/business-news/ workplace/sewage-smells-rodents-shabby-carpets-uk-workplace-2019336029/ (archived at https://perma.cc/2HPS-LVVZ)

Brown, J (2021) Half of remote workers monitored by employer staying logged on longer than necessary, research finds, People Management, 9 April. www. peoplemanagement.co.uk/news/articles/Half-remote-workers-staying-logged-on-longer-than-necessary-because-of-surveillance-research-finds#gref (archived at https://perma.cc/D5G7-7J3S)

Diver, K (2021) Why we introduced a hybrid model of flexible working at Wise, Wise, 26 January. www.wise.jobs/2021/01/26/hybrid-model-of-flexible-working-at-transferwise/ (archived at https://perma.cc/VM3S-Z8FZ)

Dodd, V (2020) Remote-working compliance YouGov survey, Skillcast, 25 November. www.skillcast.com/blog/remote-working-compliance-survey-key-findings (archived at https://perma.cc/88WQ-J9GC)

Futurism (2019) Globally, most workers think robots couldn't handle their jobs, 19 January. https://futurism.com/robots-automation-survey (archived at https://perma.cc/NC27-NMS2)

Graeber, D (2018) *Bullshit Jobs: A theory*, Simon & Schuster, New York

Issa, A (2020) Remote working is not going away: Who wins and loses when workers stay home? *Guardian*, 5 March. www.theguardian.com/lifeandstyle/2020/jul/06/remote-working-is-not-going-away-who-wins-and-loses-when-workers-stay-home (archived at https://perma.cc/3N7Z-44F6)

Jacobs, E (2021) The battle over the future of work is about autonomy, *Financial Times*, 29 August. www.ft.com/content/a0312d93-5ae9-4945-b990-6f3fd7a880cf (archived at https://perma.cc/UK96-UKQV)

Kakkad, J, Palmou, C, Britto, D and Browne, J (2021) Anywhere jobs: Reshaping the geography of work, Tony Blair Institute for Global Change, 16 June. https://institute.global/policy/anywhere-jobs-reshaping-geography-work (archived at https://perma.cc/6UMW-YBDT)

Kotkin, J (2020) *The Coming of Neo-Feudalism: A warning to the global middle class*, Encounter Books, New York

Magdalena, S, Wood, A J and Burchell, B (2021) Alienation is not 'bullshit': An empirical critique of Graeber's theory of BS jobs, *Work, Employment and Society*, 2 June. https://journals.sagepub.com/doi/full/10.1177/09500170211015067 (archived at https://perma.cc/XS4V-JHM7)

Nakamichi, T and Taniguchi, T (2021) Nakamishi Nomura tells staff not to smoke cigarettes when working from home, Bloomberg, 1 September. www.bloomberg.com/news/articles/2021-09-01/nomura-tells-staff-don-t-smoke-during-work-hours-even-at-home (archived at https://perma.cc/8JSZ-CCRY)

National Accident Helpline (2021) Working from home accidents, 7 January. www.national-accident-helpline.co.uk/news/post/working-home-accidents (archived at https://perma.cc/AE8M-BTHL)

Pew Research Center (2017) Americans' attitudes toward a future in which robots and computers can do many human jobs, 4 October. www.pewresearch.org/internet/2017/10/04/americans-attitudes-toward-a-future-in-which-robots-and-computers-can-do-many-human-jobs/ (archived at https://perma.cc/KHU8-TPVE)

Prospect (2021) *Hybrid Working and the Right to Disconnect*, April. https://library. prospect.org.uk/id/2021/00381?display=authoritypdf&revision=1 (archived at https://perma.cc/5Y9H-J5Z7)

Reeves, R (2020) In this new post-coronavirus world, one day of menstrual leave a month is all I ask, *Independent*, 21 June. www.independent.co.uk/voices/ coronavirus-menstrual-leave-periods-working-home-tampon-tax-a9576241. html (archived at https://perma.cc/F5GW-3BFT)

Romano, F (2011) The day the typesetting industry died, What They Think, 16 December. https://whattheythink.com/articles/55522-day-typesetting-industry-died/ (archived at https://perma.cc/JY22-2K9Q)

Sanchez, S (2021) PHD: Marketers spend more time reporting than creating, *Campaign*, 18 August. www.campaignlive.co.uk/article/phd-marketers-spend-time-reporting-creating/1725097 (archived at https://perma.cc/3RNN-L7X7)

SAP and Qualtrics (2019) *Globalization 4.0: The human experience*, January. www3.weforum.org/docs/WEF_globalization4_Jan18.pdf (archived at https:// perma.cc/H4EB-ZC6F)

Conclusion

Hughes, O (2021) Remote work is making productivity and innovation harder, says Microsoft study, ZDNet. 13 September. www.zdnet.com/article/remote-work-is-making-productivity-and-innovation-harder-says-microsoft-study/ (archived at https://perma.cc/5P77-DFVX)

KFC (2020) And the winner of the award for the most inappropriate slogan for 2020 goes to... KFC, Yum! Limited Press Office, 24 August. https://global.kfc. com/press-releases/and-the-winner-of-the-award-for-the-most-inappropriate-slogan-for-2020-goes-to-kfc (archived at https://perma.cc/Q6L2-KKHG)

McKinsey (2020) What's next for remote work: An analysis of 2,000 tasks, 800 jobs, and nine countries. www.mckinsey.com/featured-insights/future-of-work/whats-next-for-remote-work-an-analysis-of-2000-tasks-800-jobs-and-nine-countries (archived at https://perma.cc/4QWU-V9GY)

Mikkelson, D (2011) Blue collar innovation, Snopes, 21 January. www.snopes.com/ fact-check/blue-collar-innovation/ (archived at https://perma.cc/HS8D-TW3R)

INDEX

CPSIA information can be obtained
at www.ICGtesting.com
Printed in the USA
LVHW071616200223
739943LV00008B/561

9 781398 603882